Azita Gandjei

MYTHOSCAPE

Daylight

Cofounder: Michael Itkoff
Creative Director: Ursula Damm
Copy Editor: Gabrielle Fastman

ISBN: 978-1-954119-37-6

Printed by Ofset Yapimevi, Turkey

Daylight Books
E-mail: info@daylightbooks.org
Web: www.daylightbooks.org

A tree ascended there. Oh pure transcendence!
Oh Orpheus sings! Oh tall tree in the ear!
And all things hushed. Yet even in that silence
a new beginning, beckoning, change appeared.

—Rainer Maria Rilke, *Sonnets to Orpheus*

One does not become enlightened by imagining figures of light, but by making the darkness conscious. The latter procedure, however, is disagreeable and therefore not popular.

—Carl Jung, *Psychology & Alchemy*

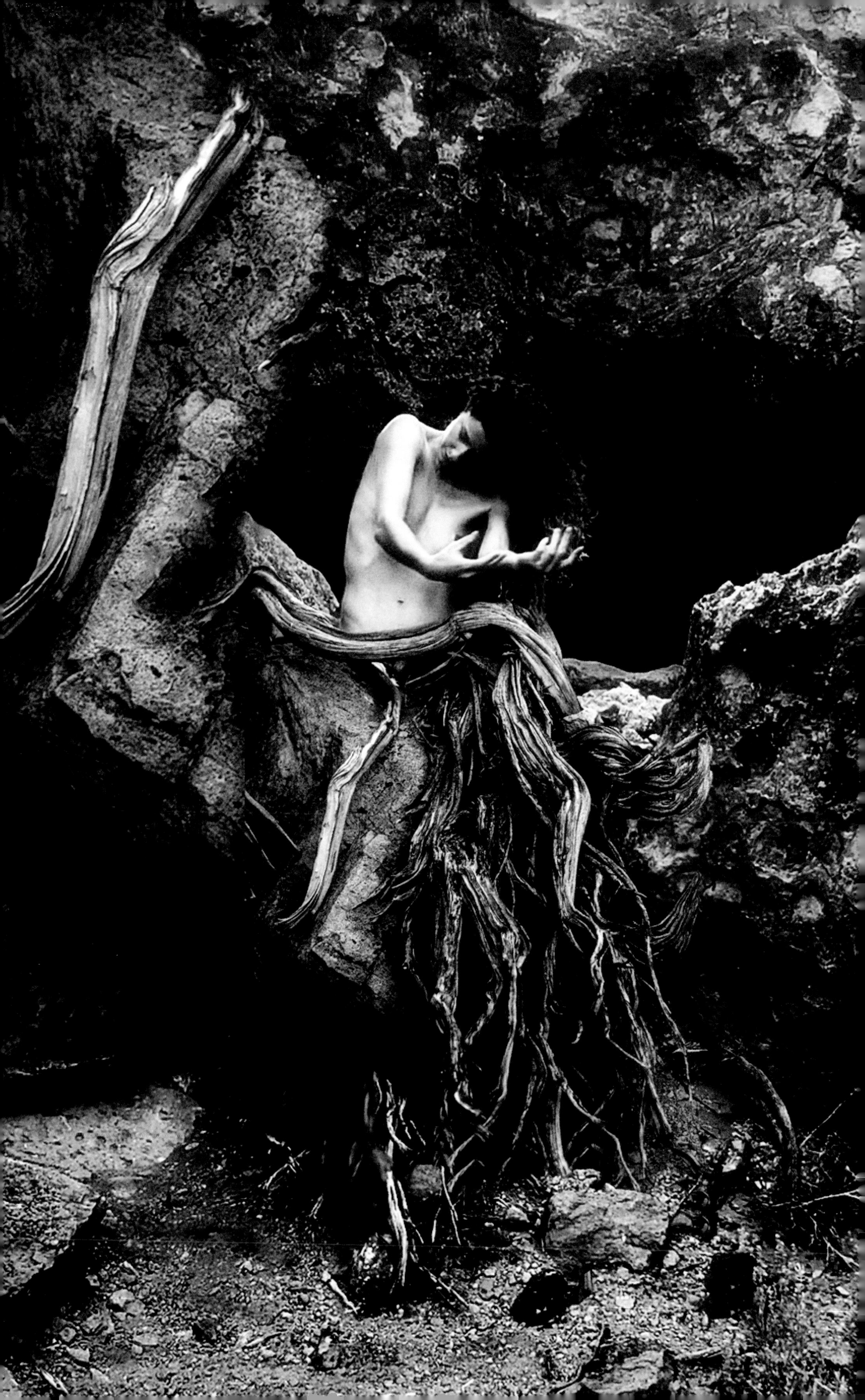

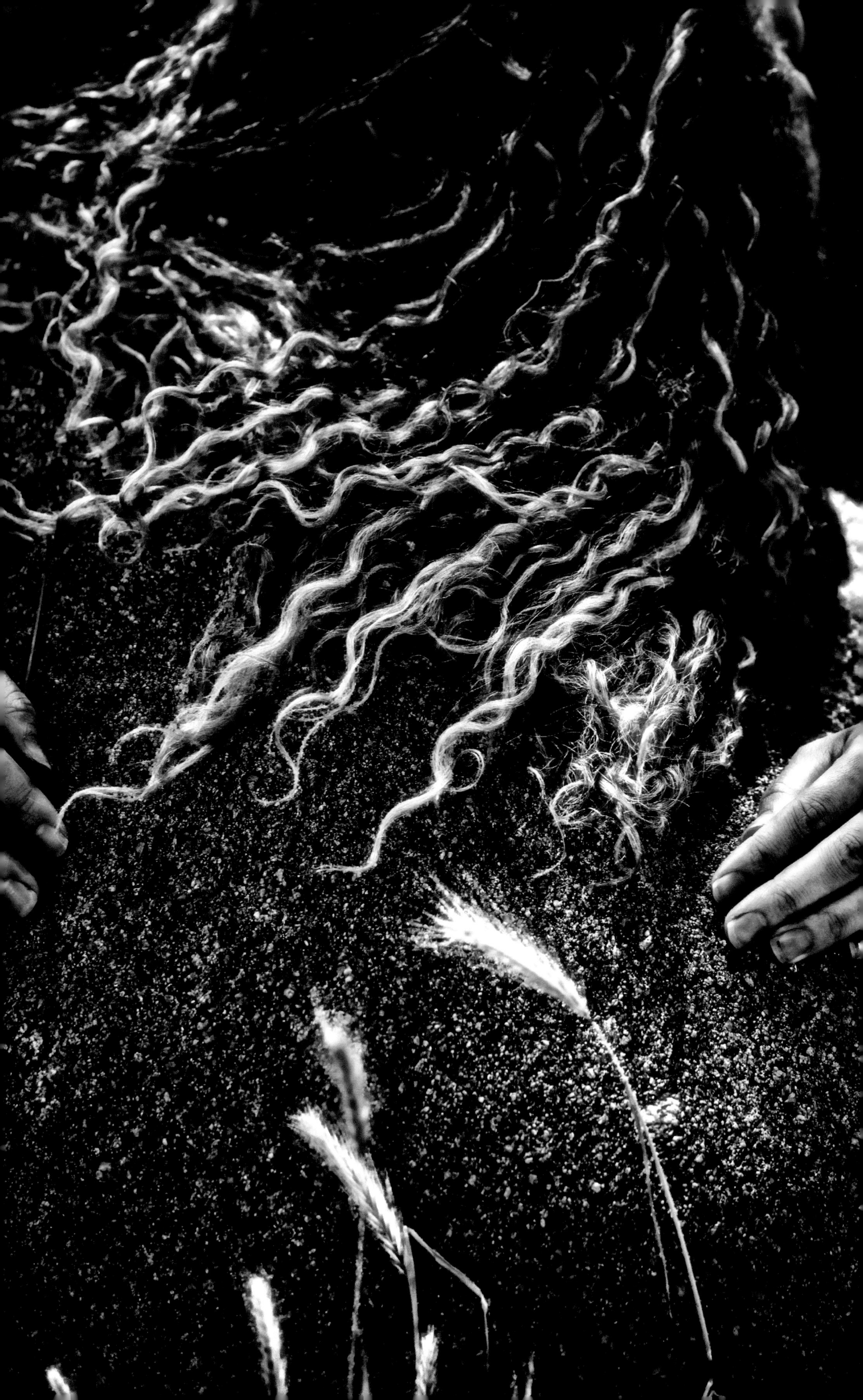

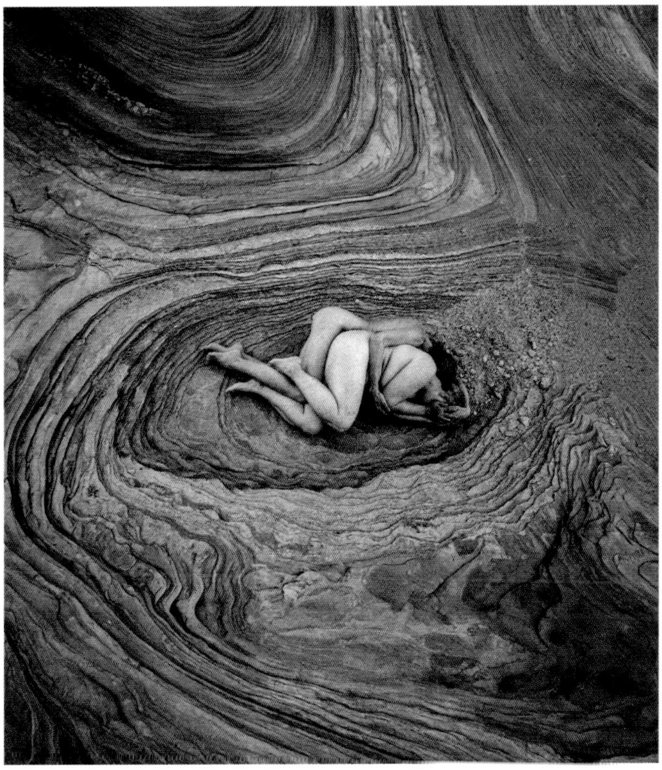

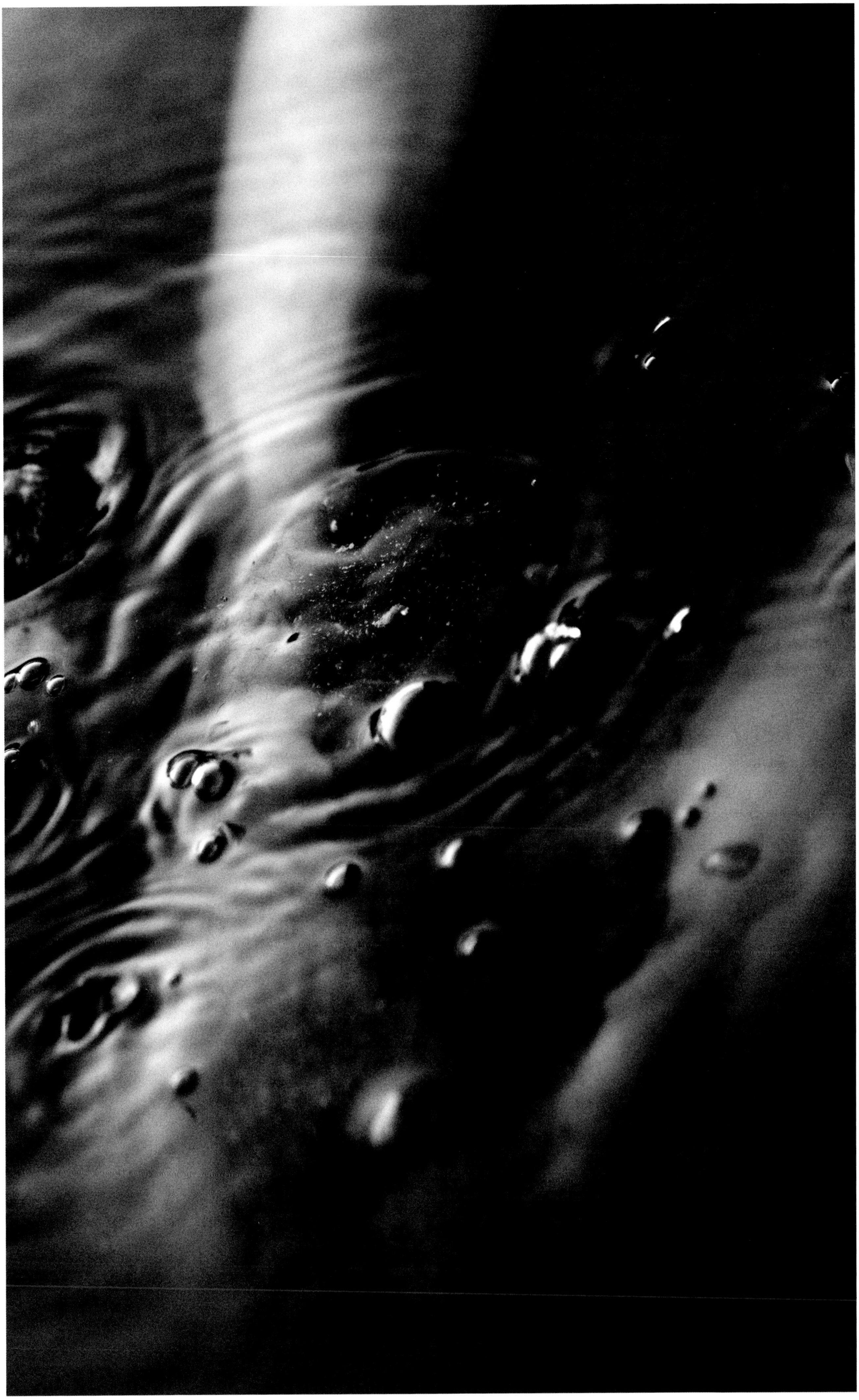

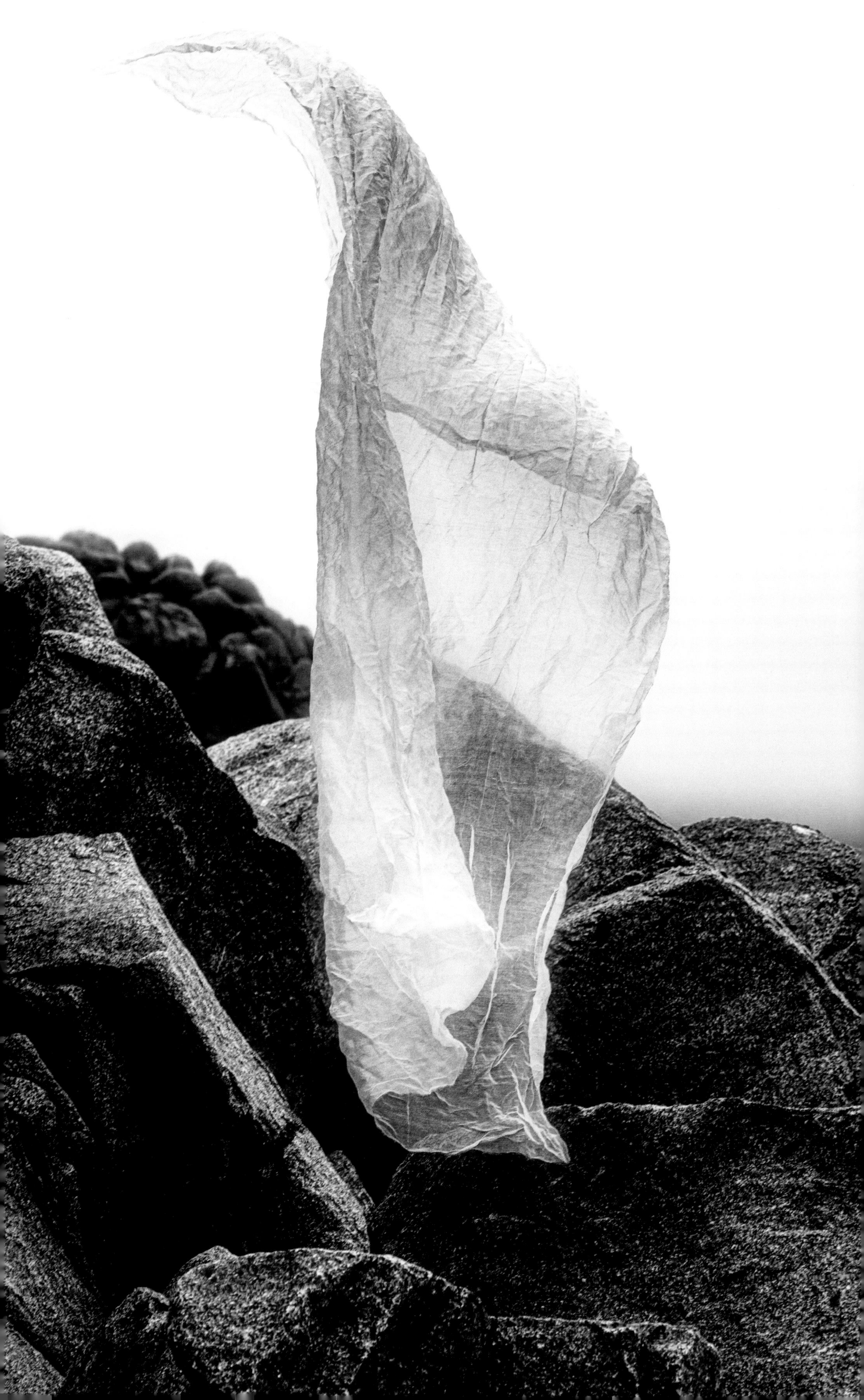

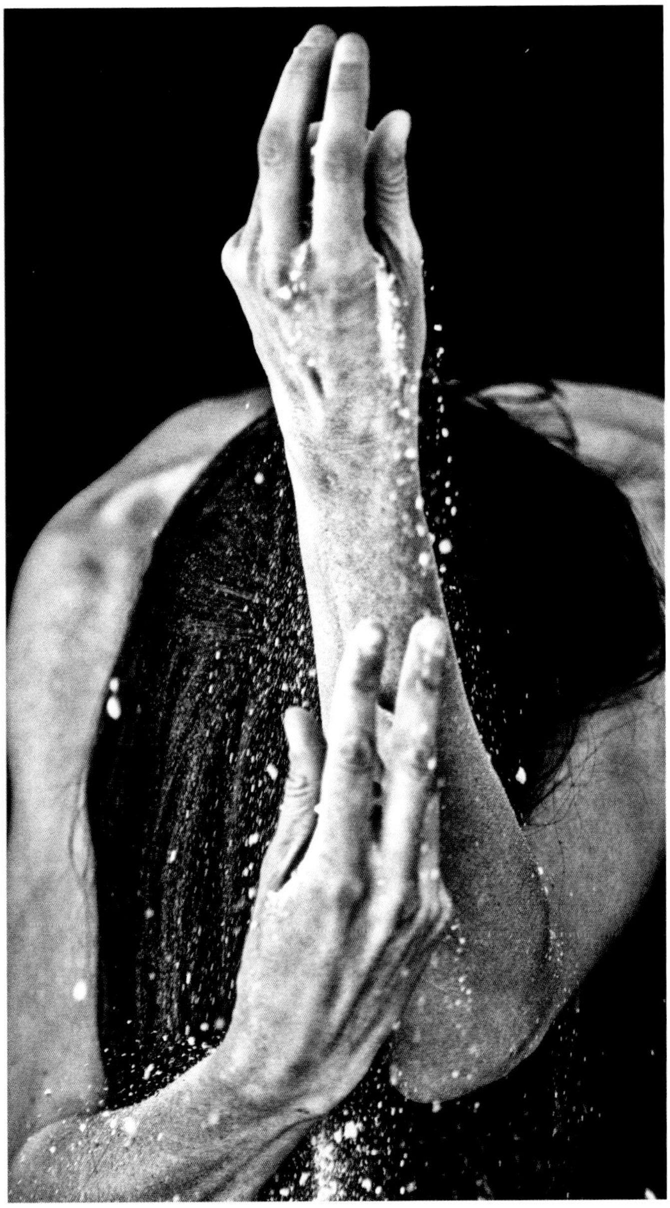

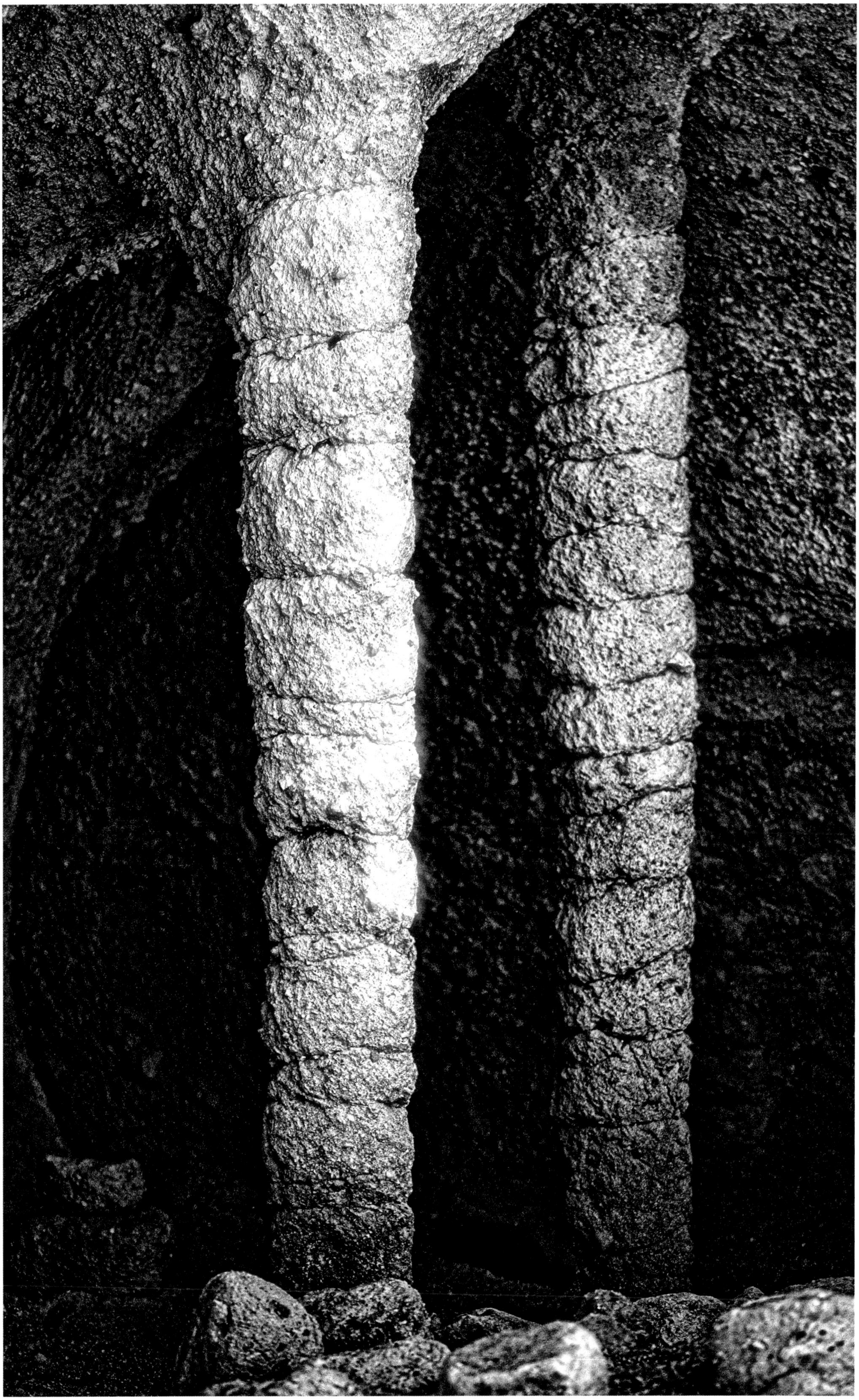

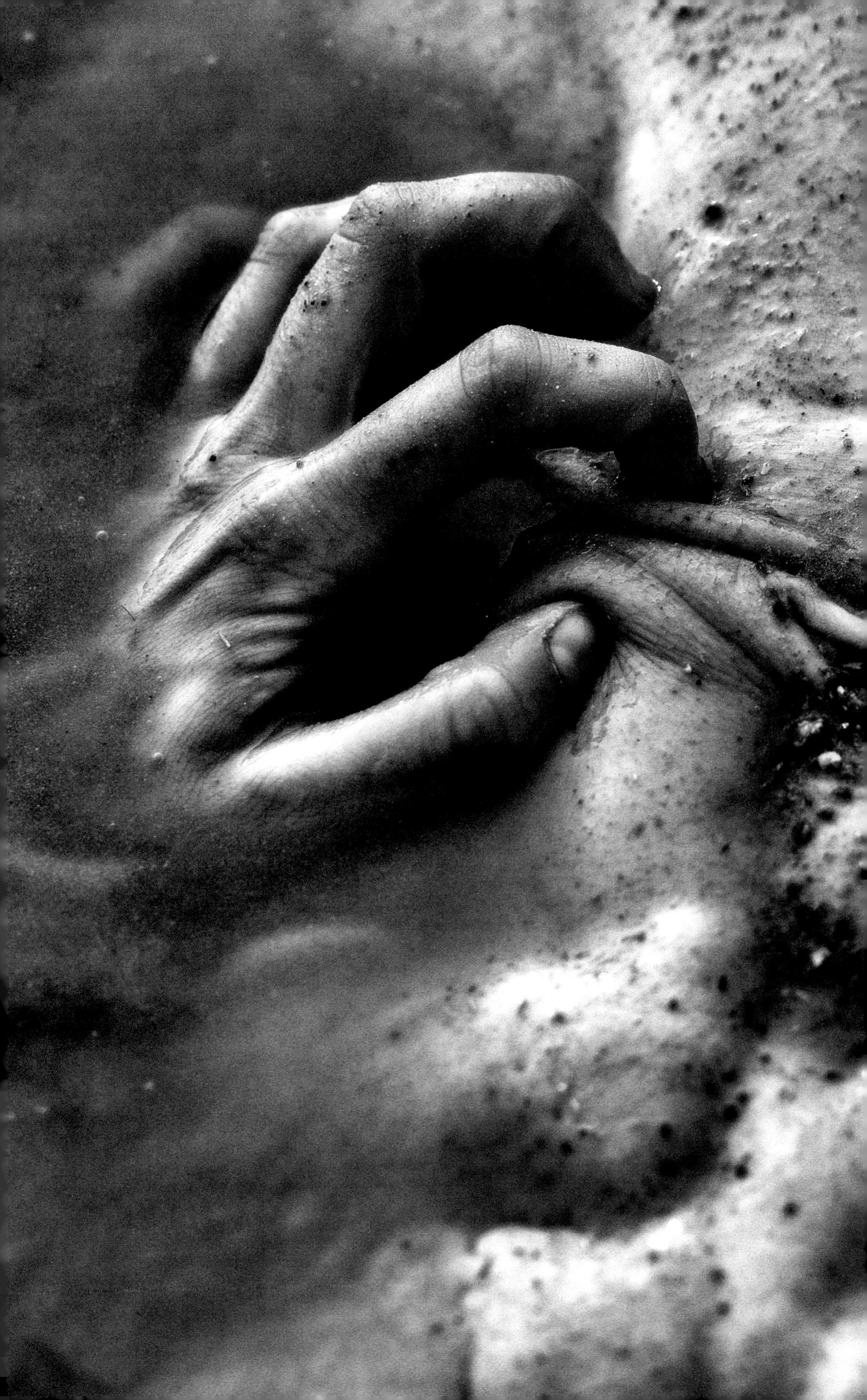

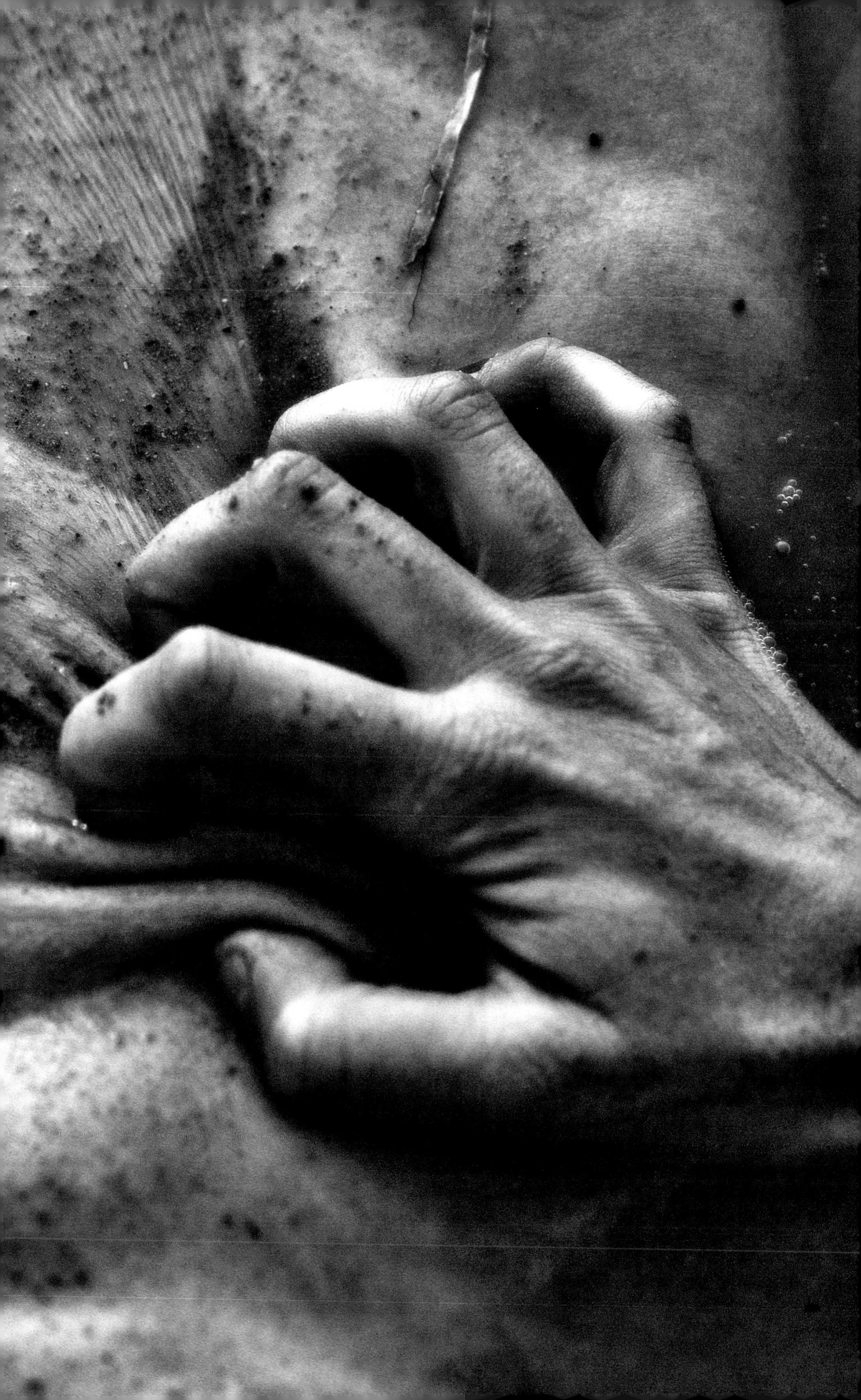

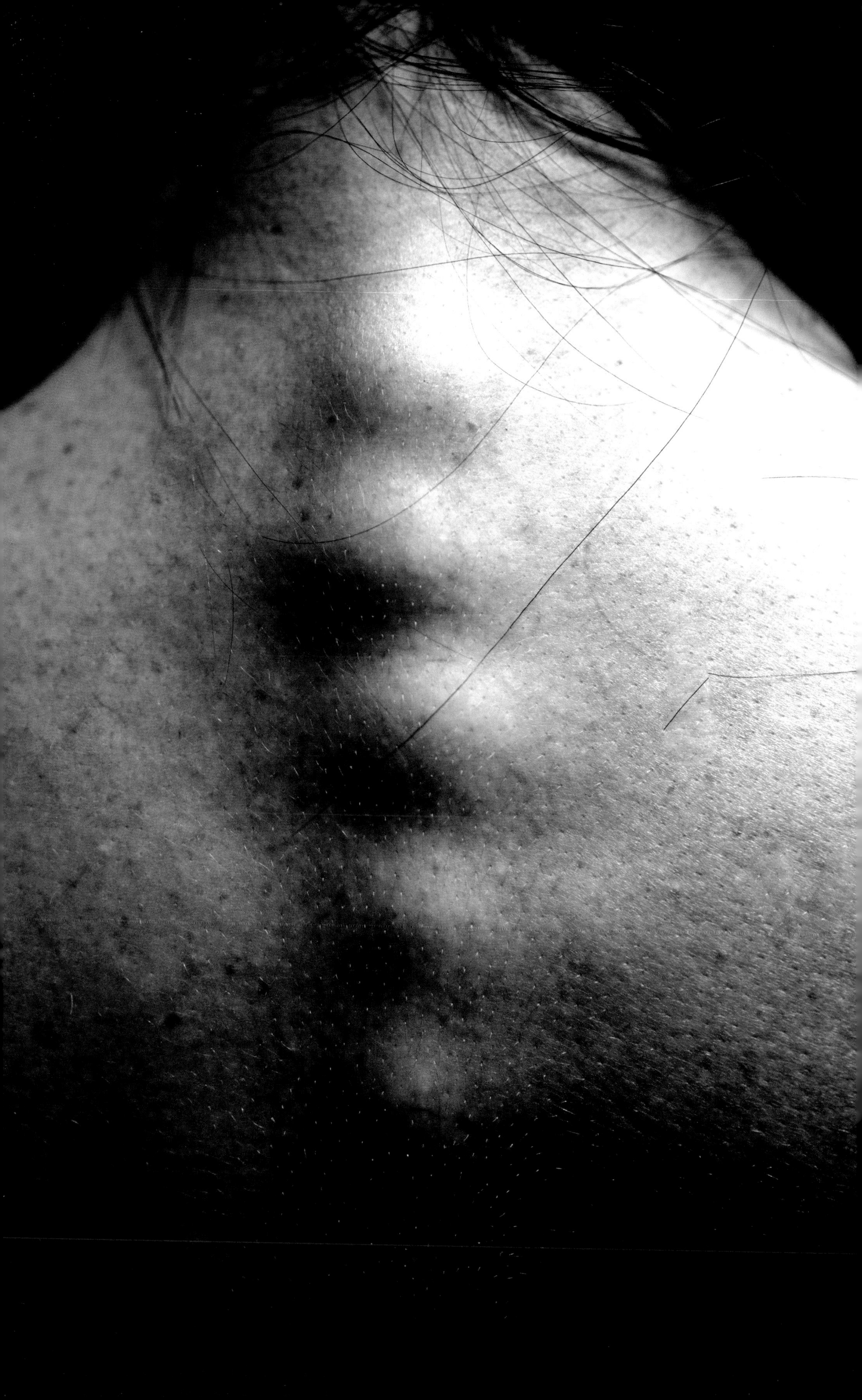

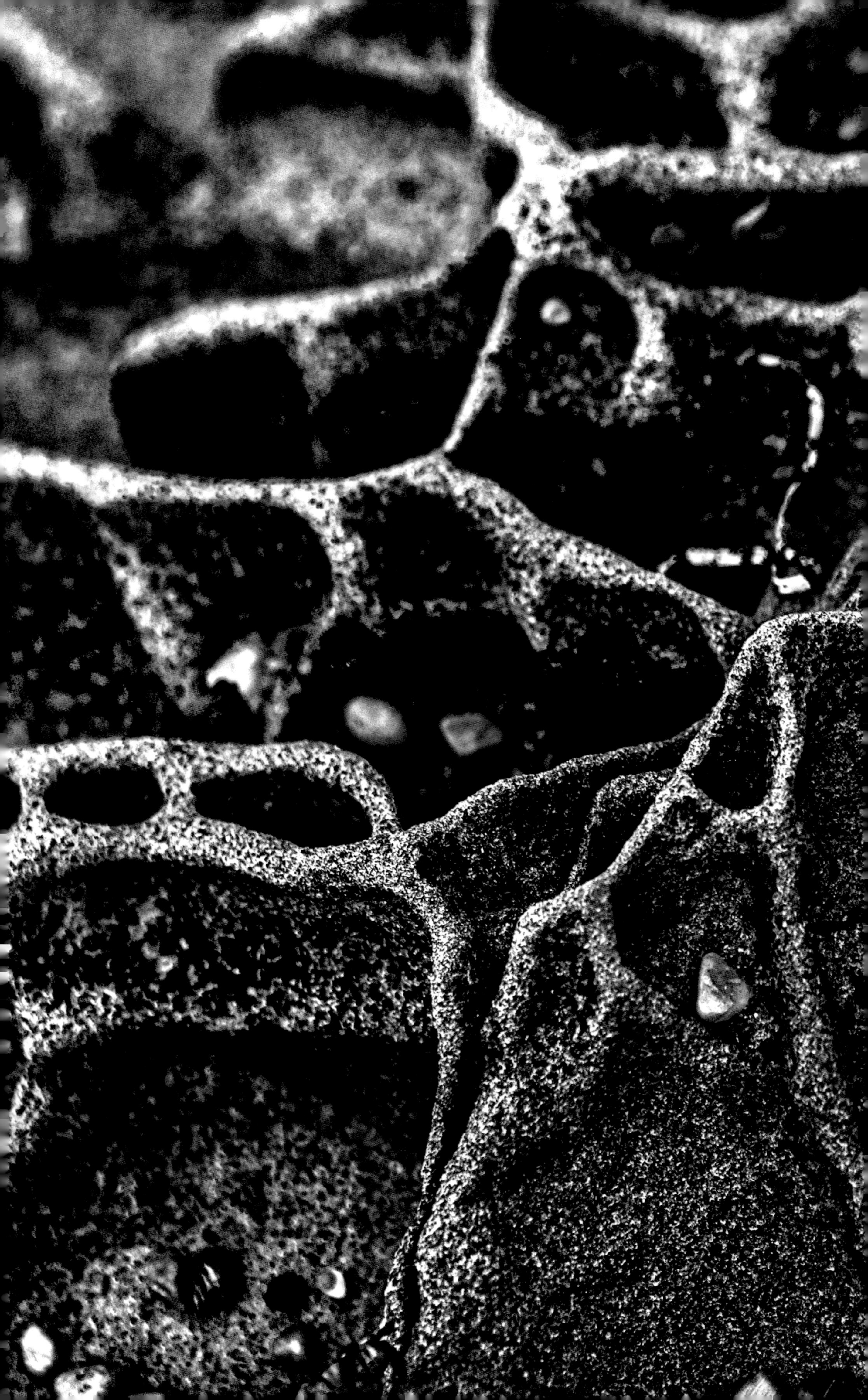

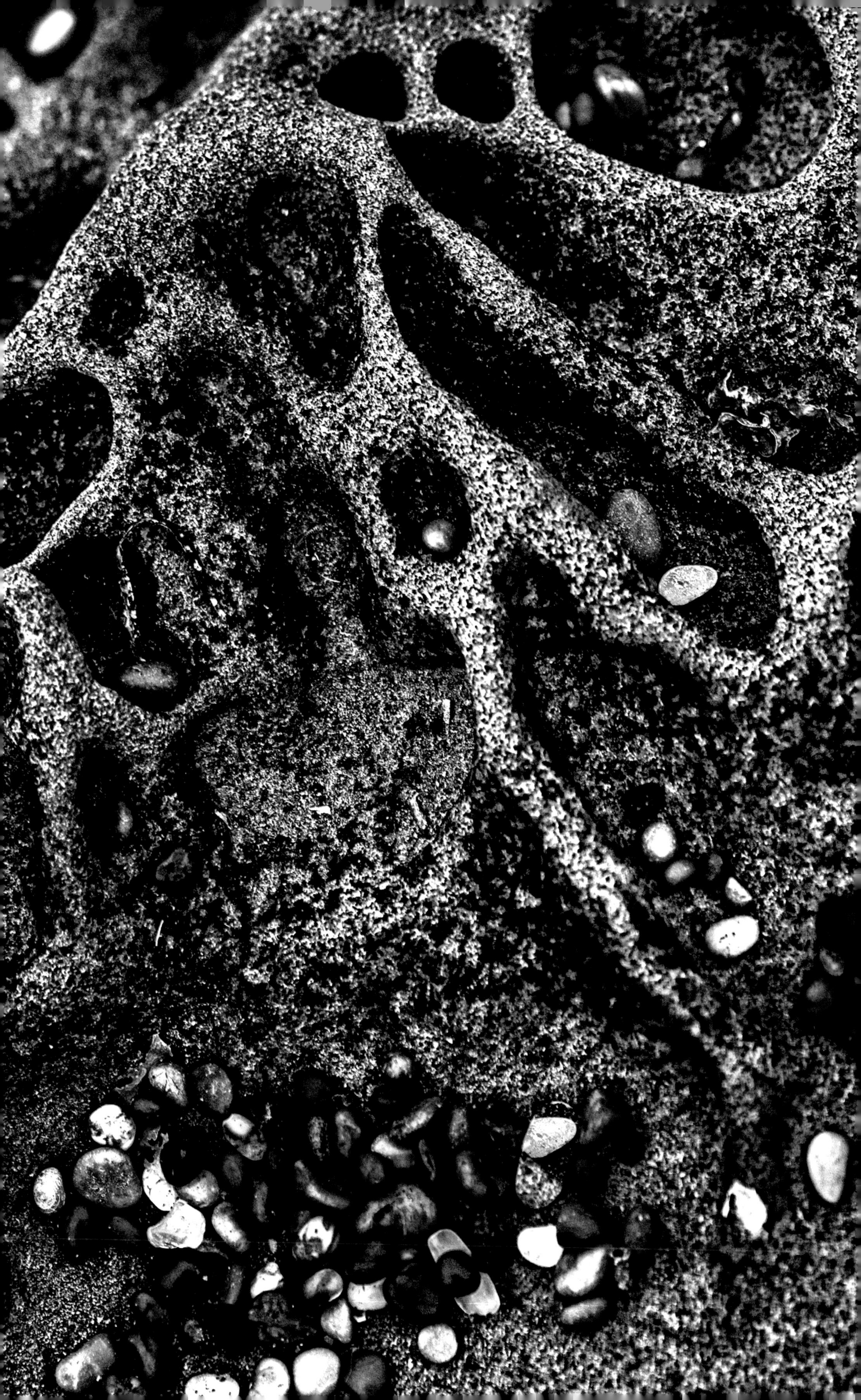

My soul leads me into the desert, into the desert of my own self. I did not think that my soul is a desert, a barren, hot desert, dusty and without drink.

—Carl Jung

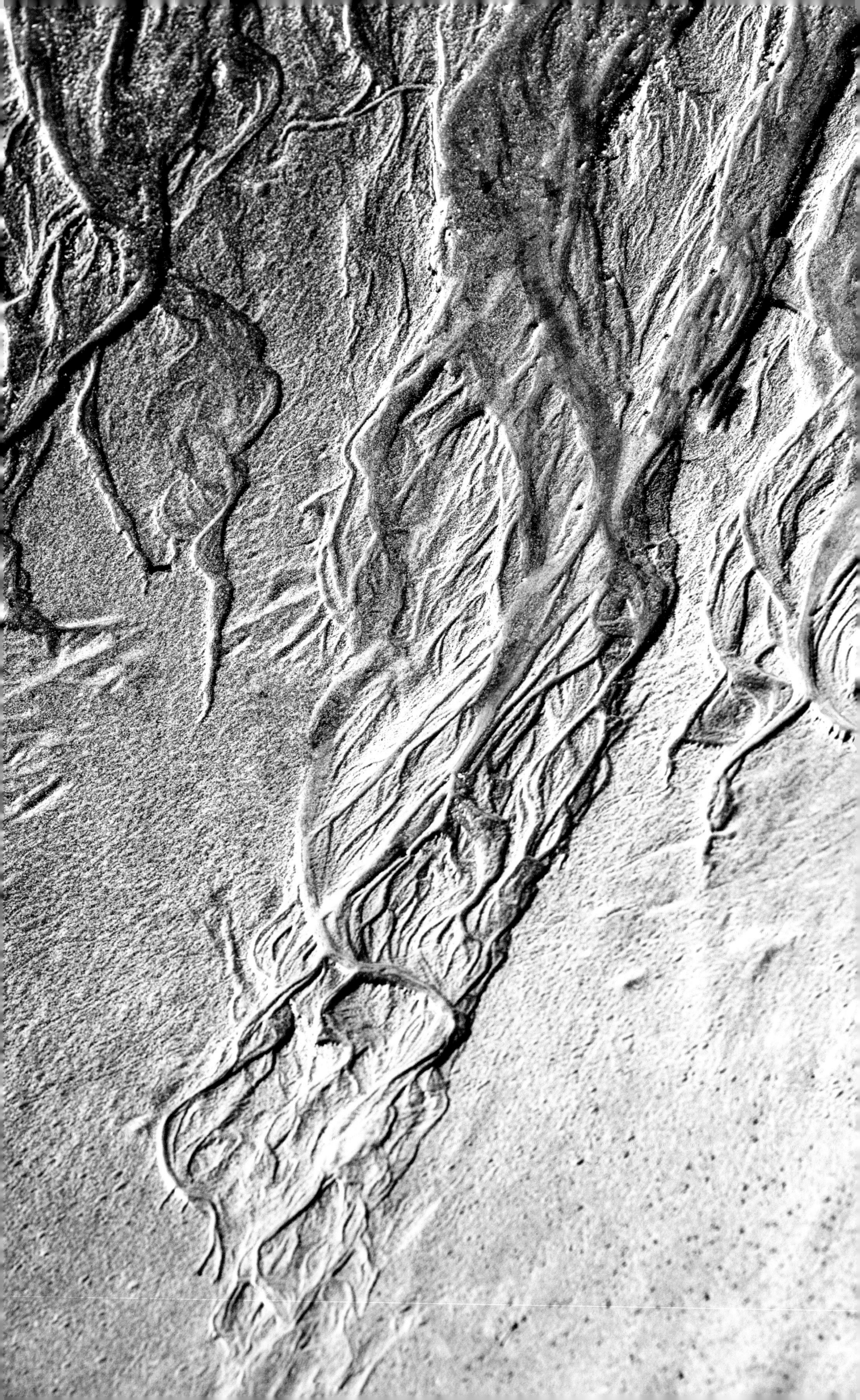

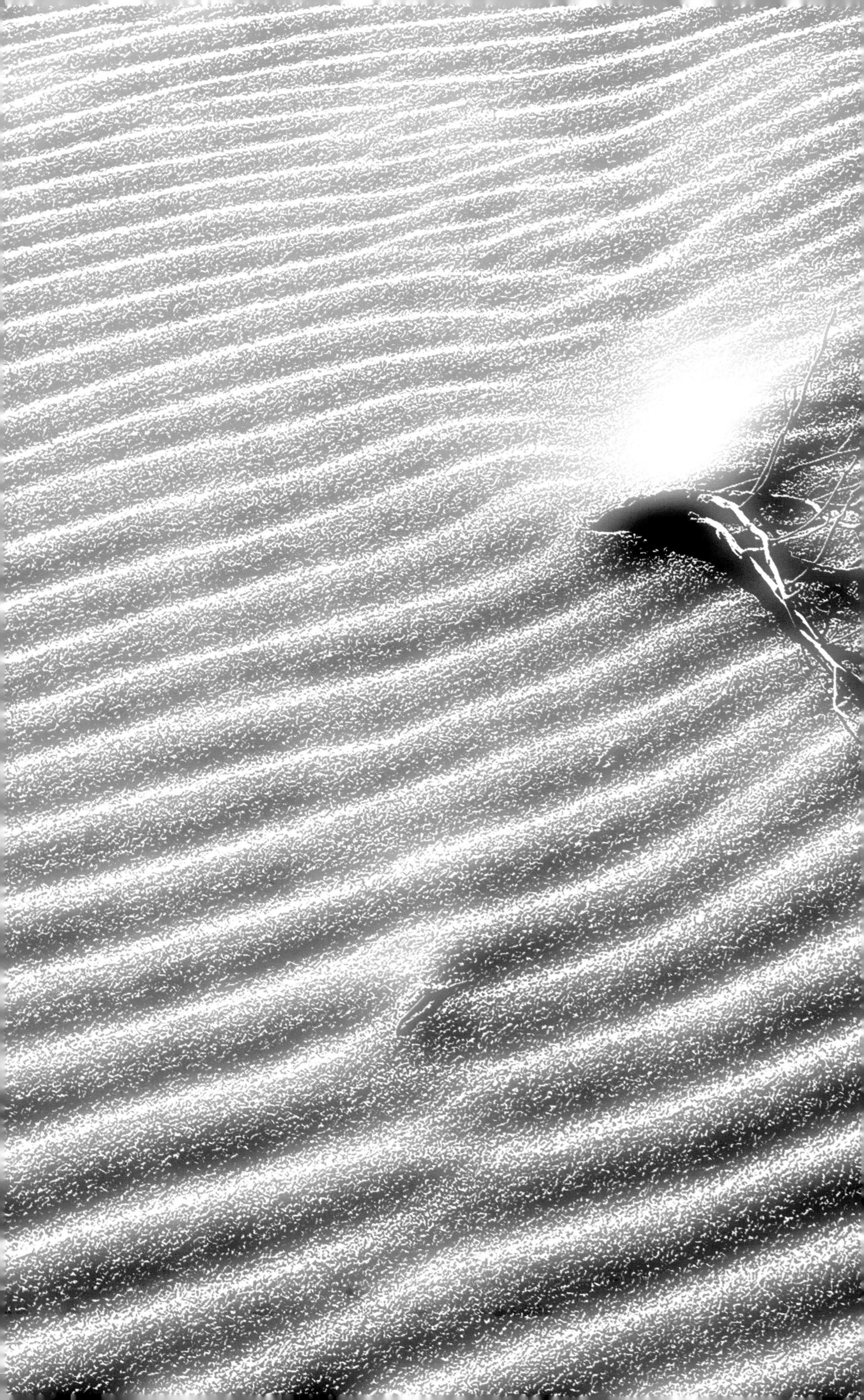

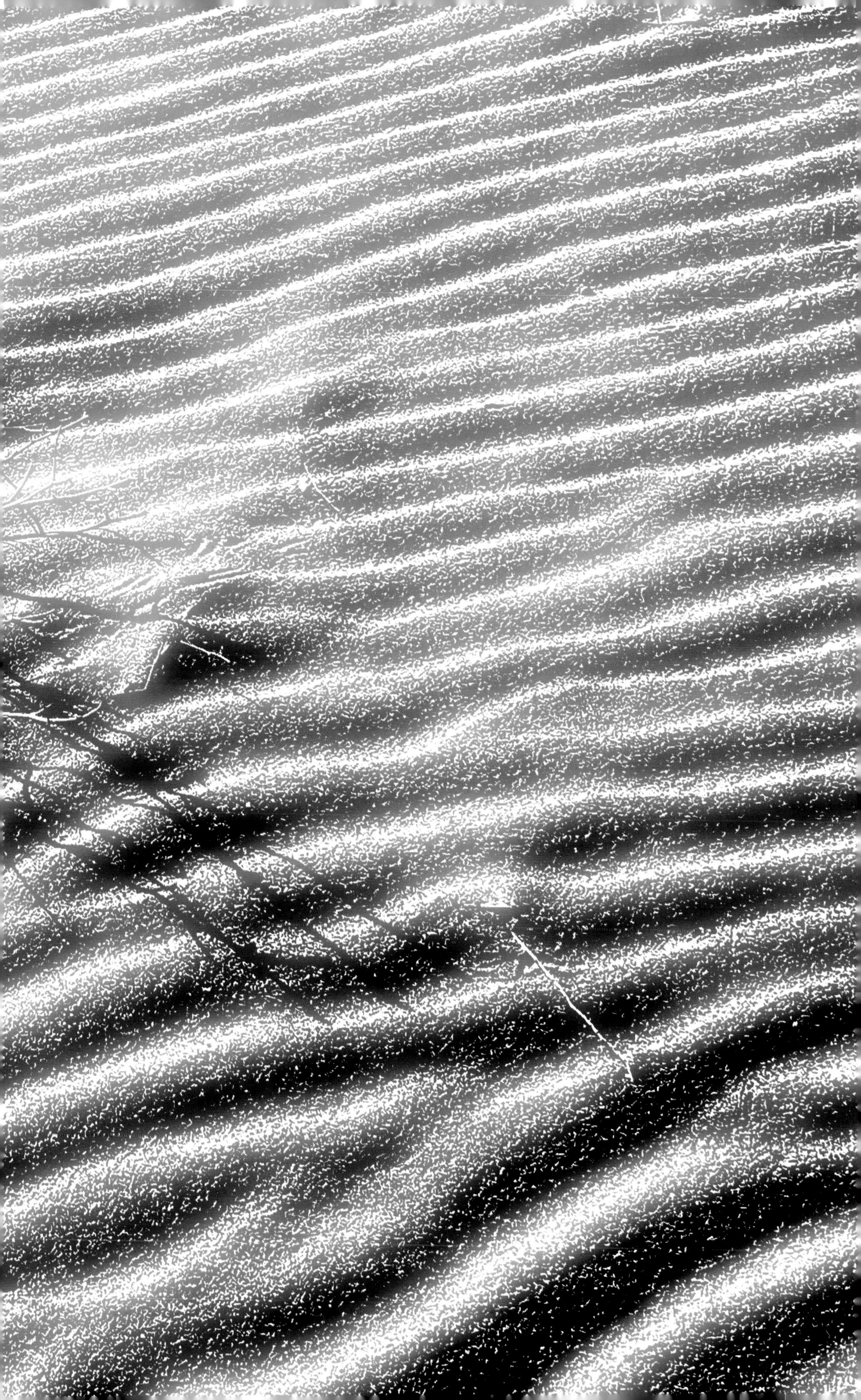

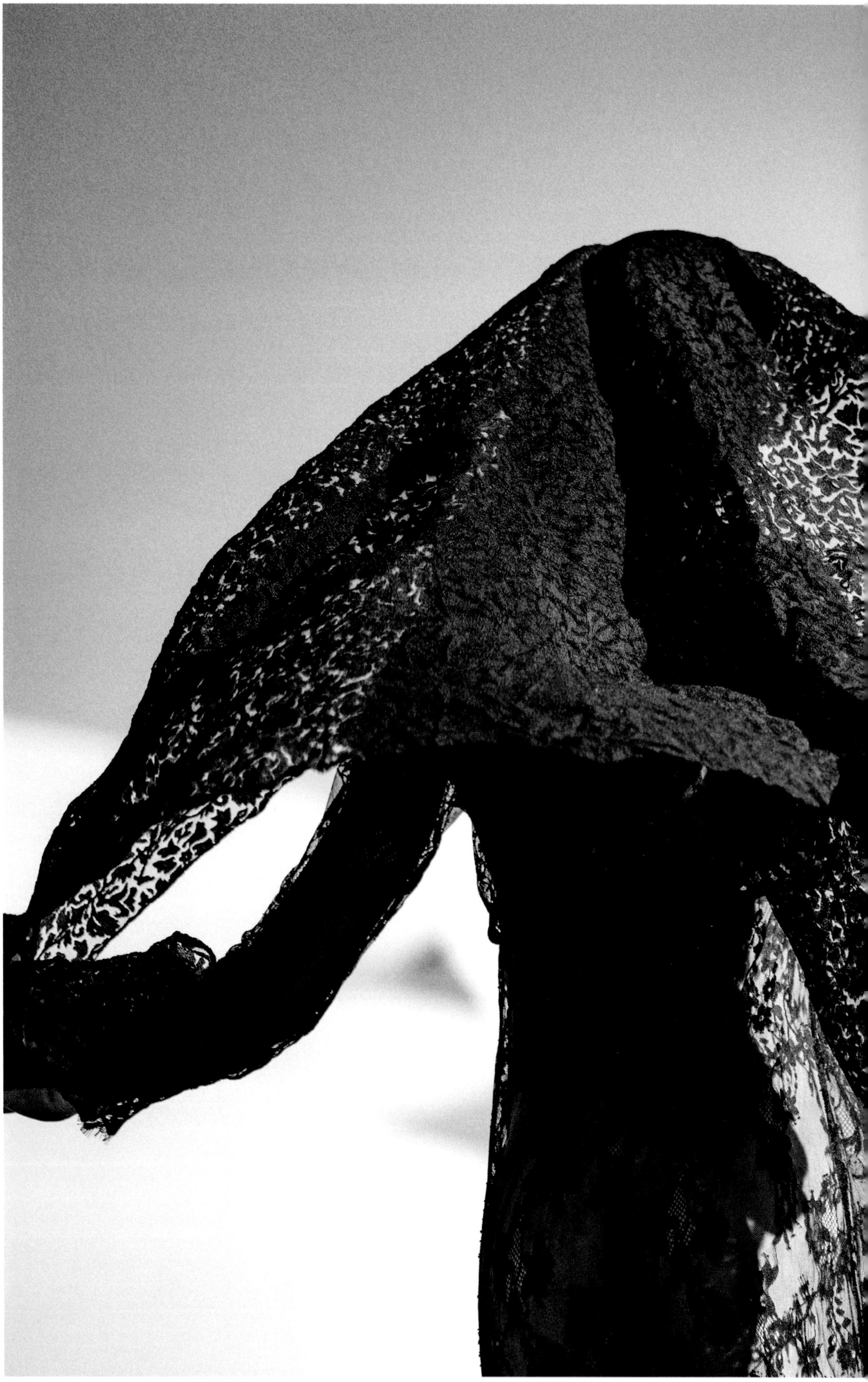

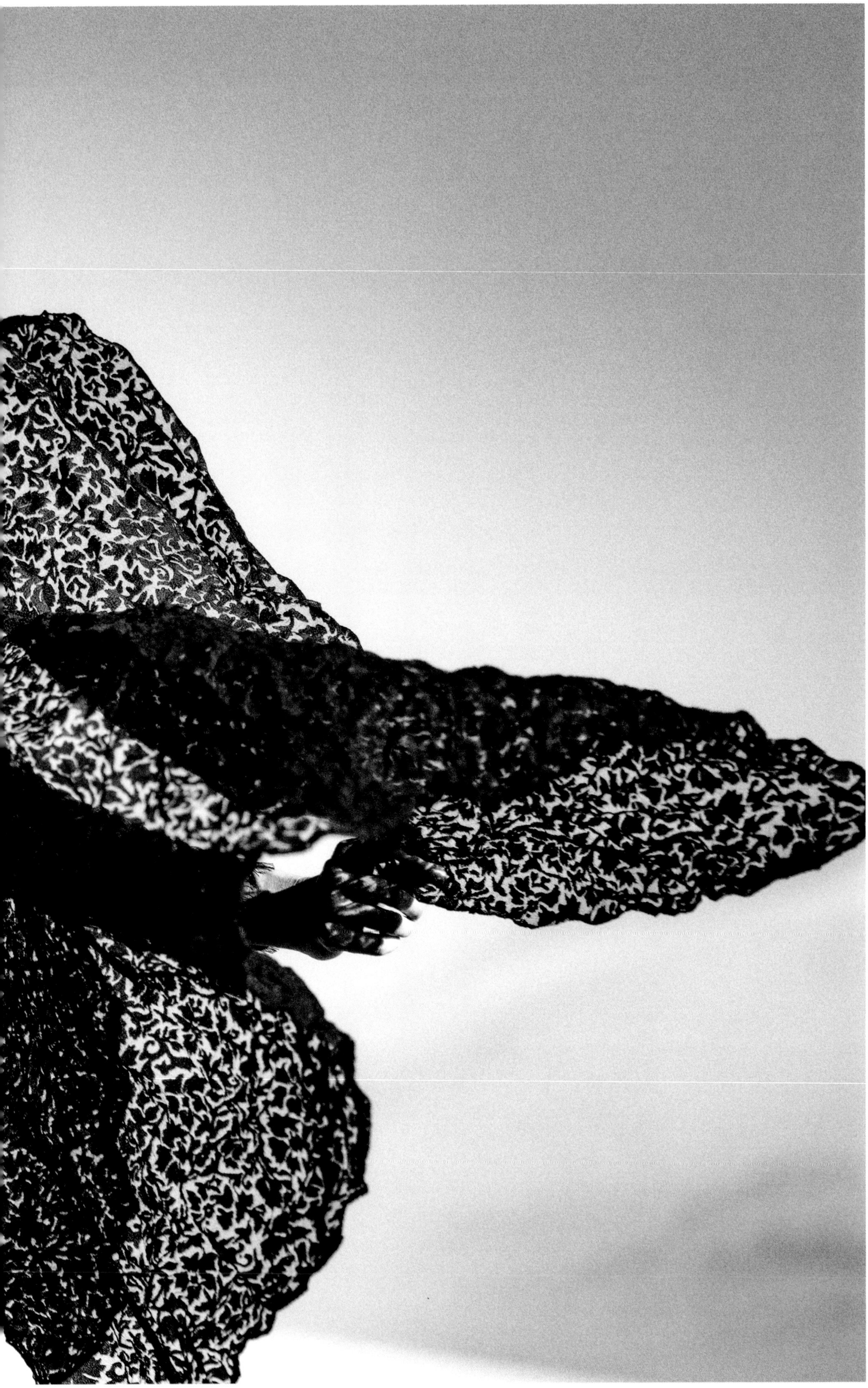

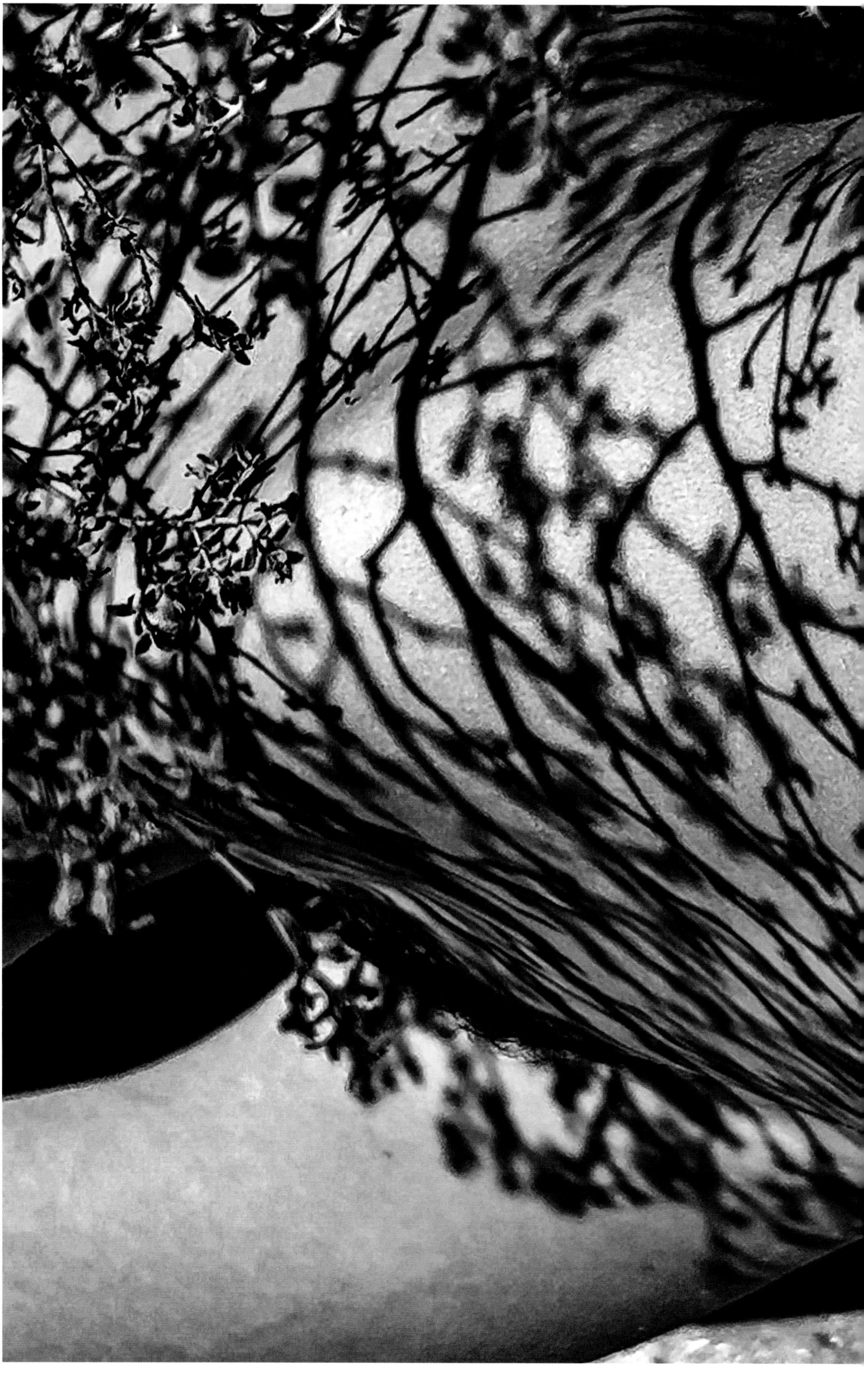

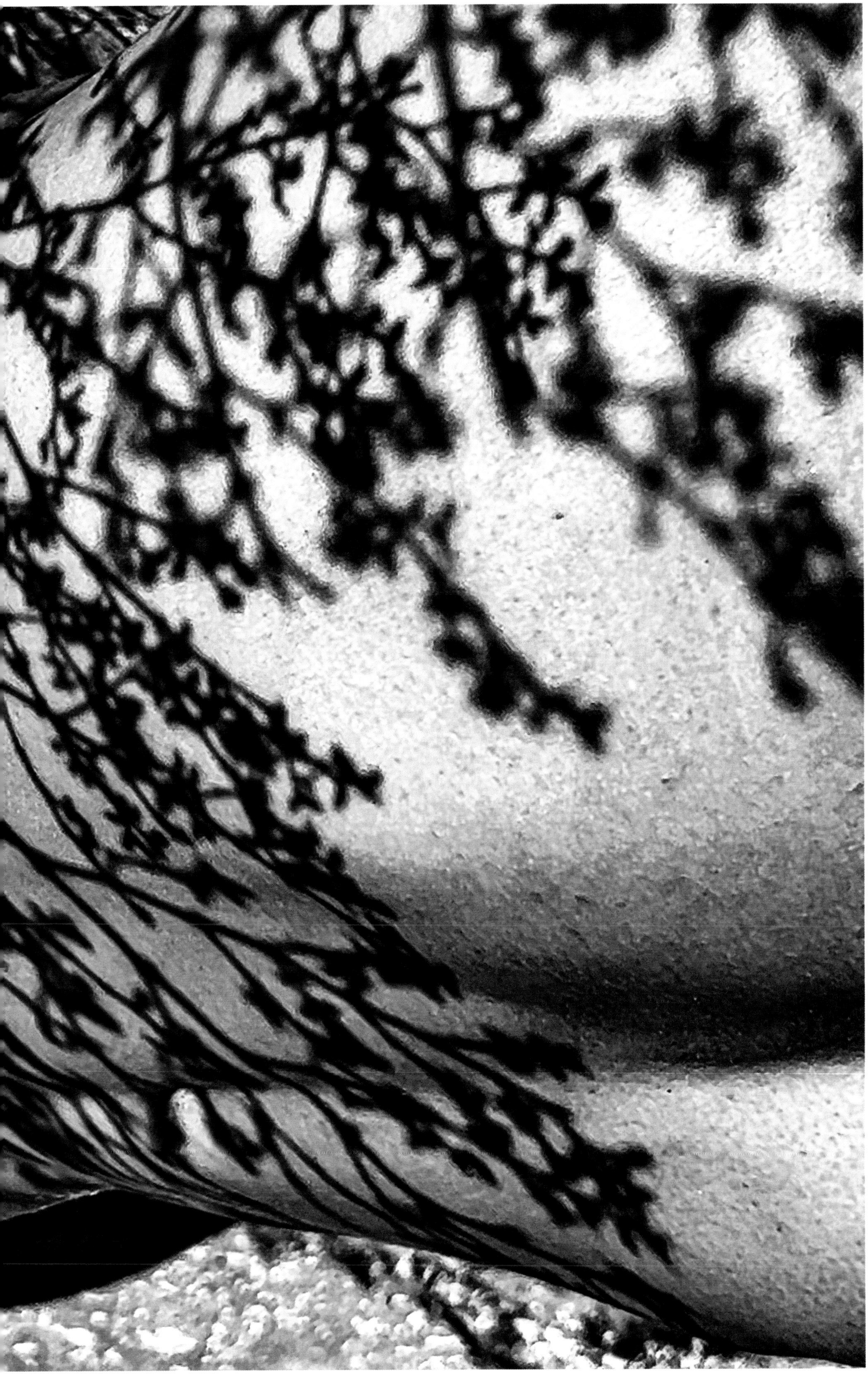

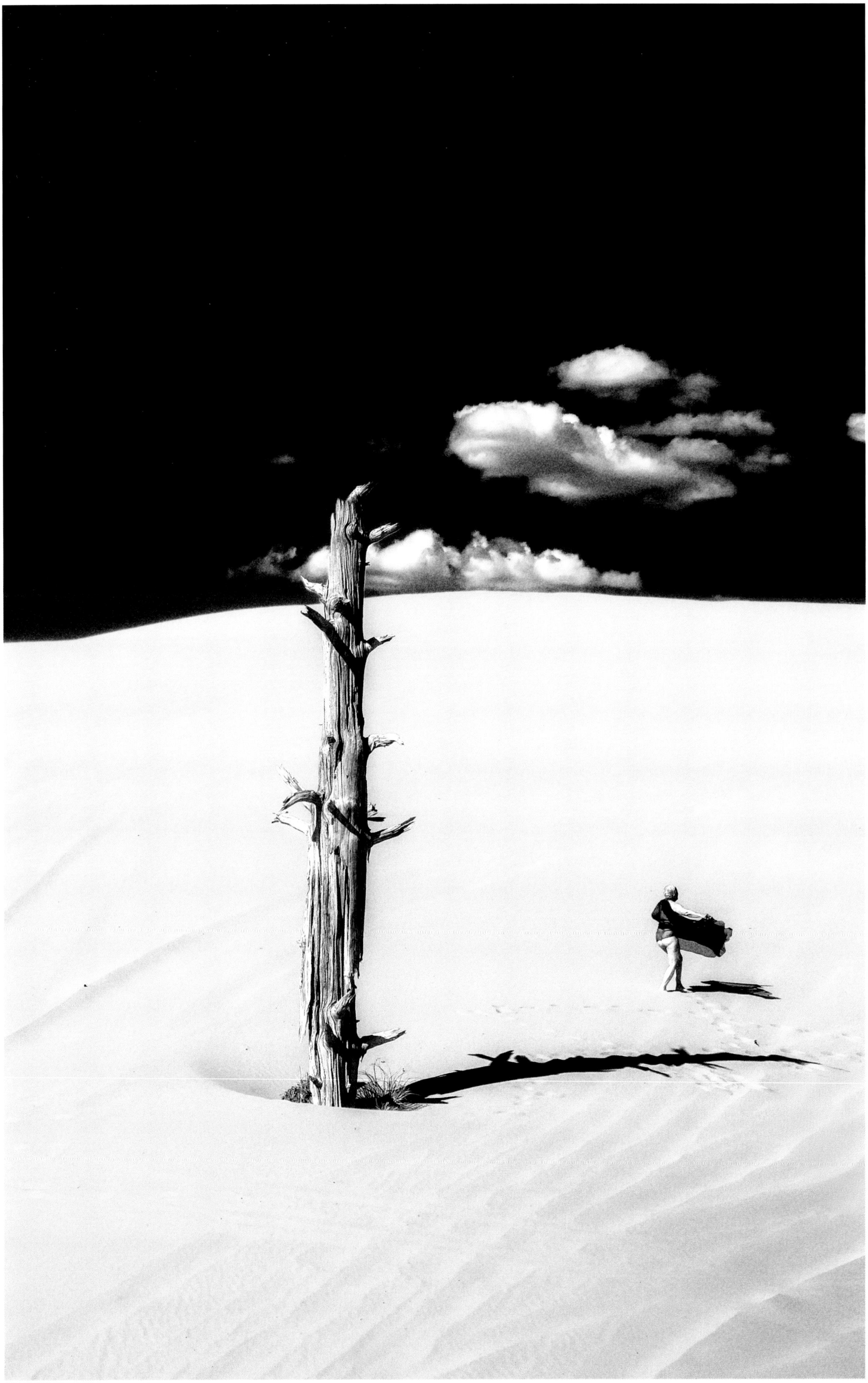

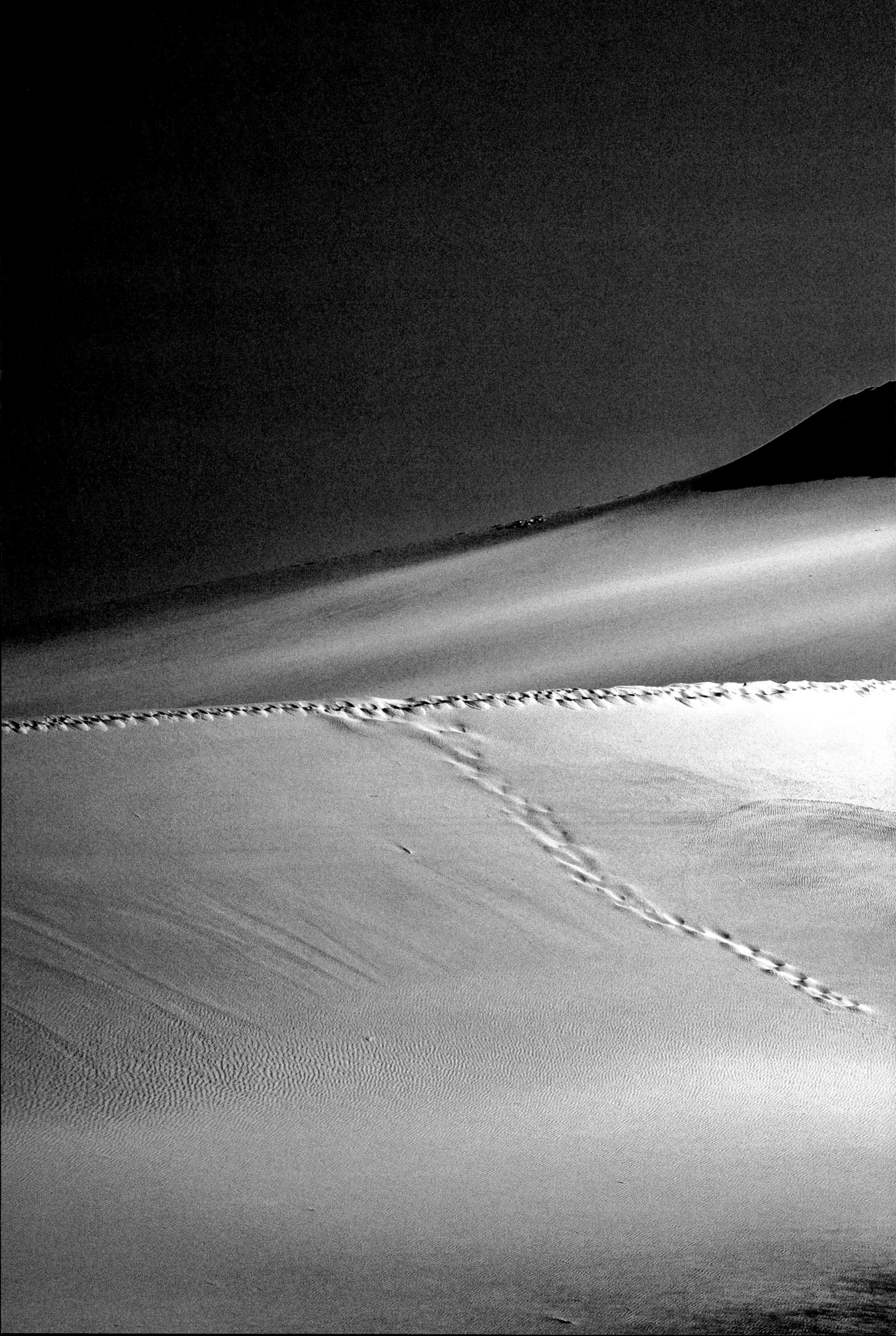

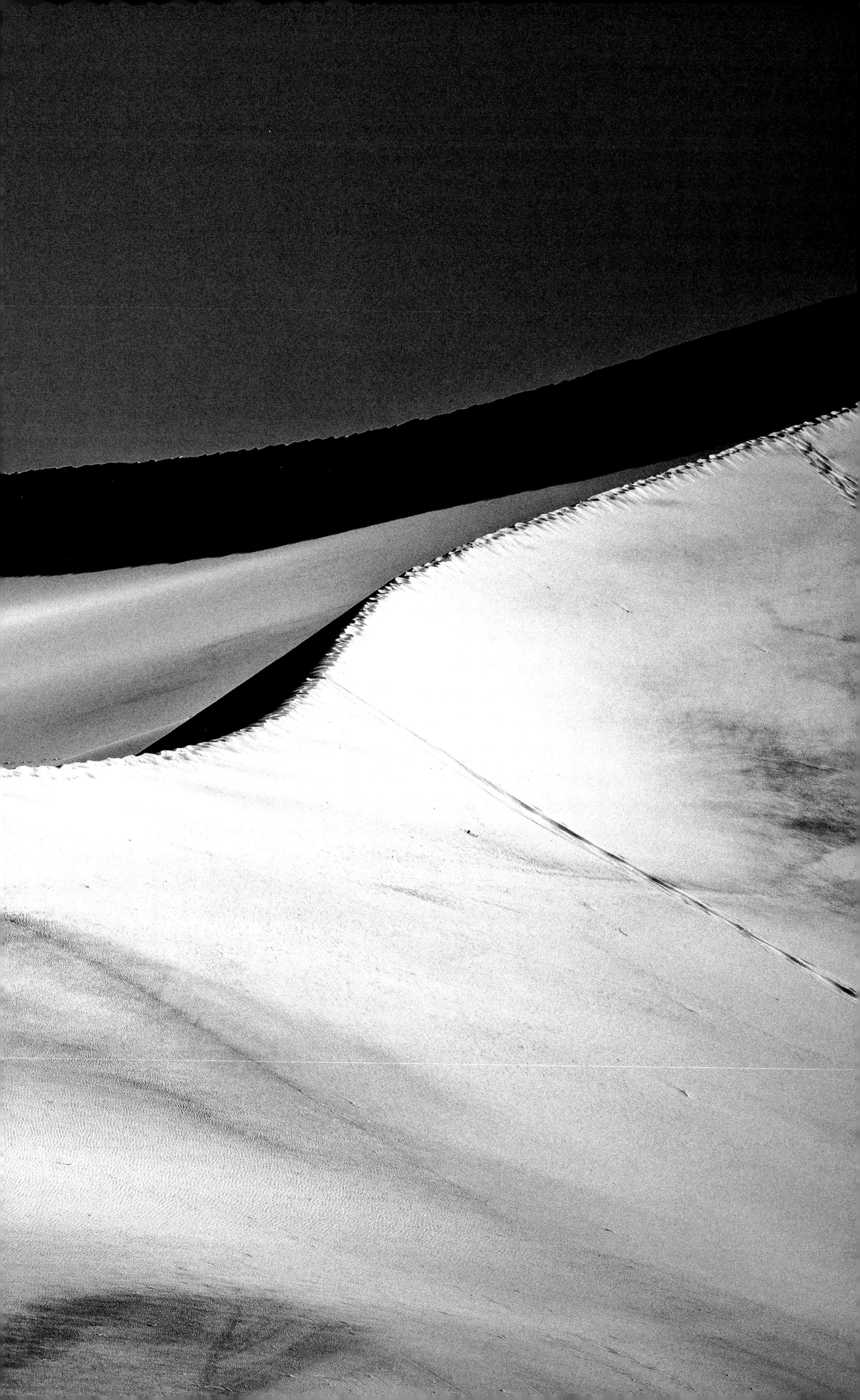

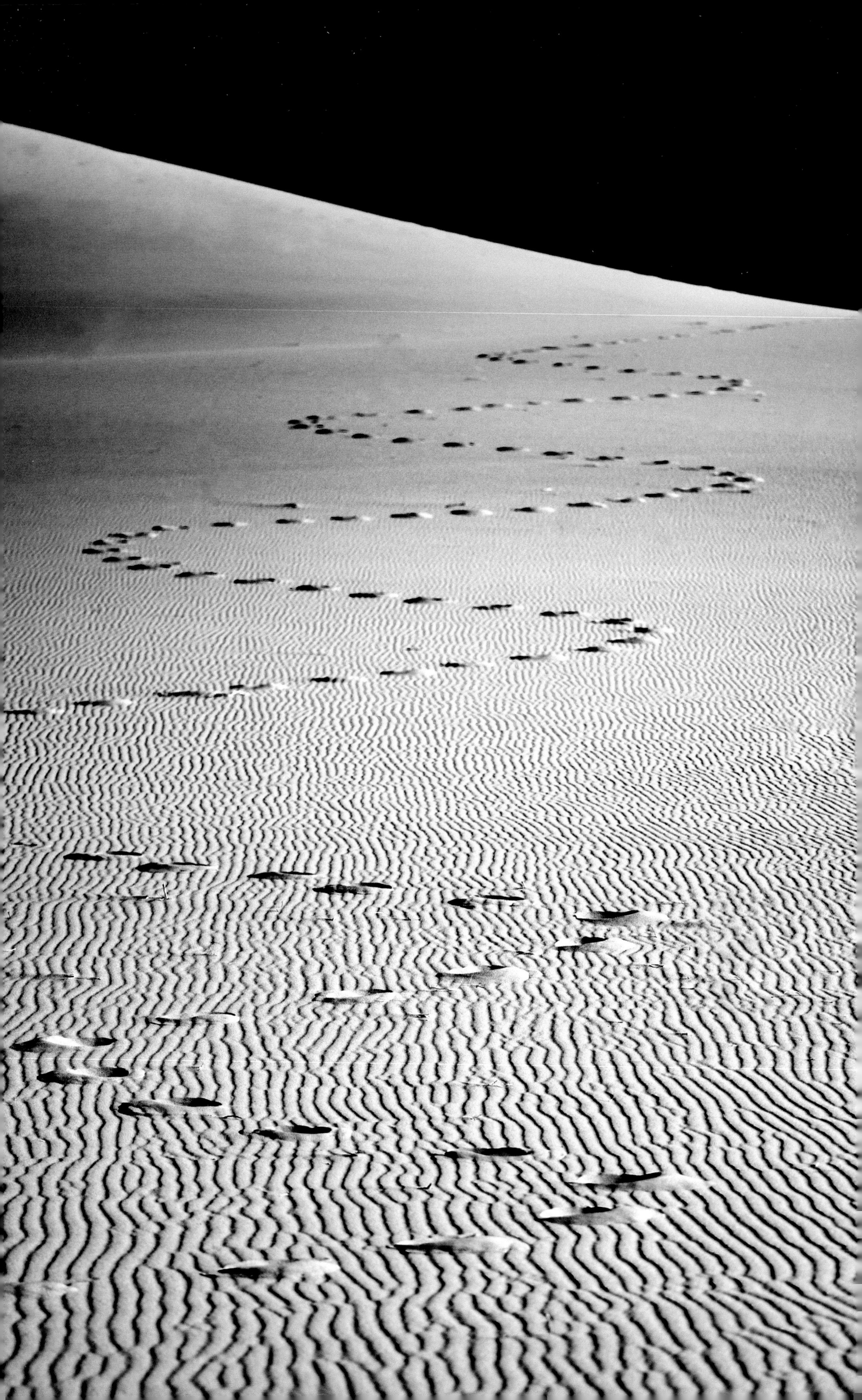

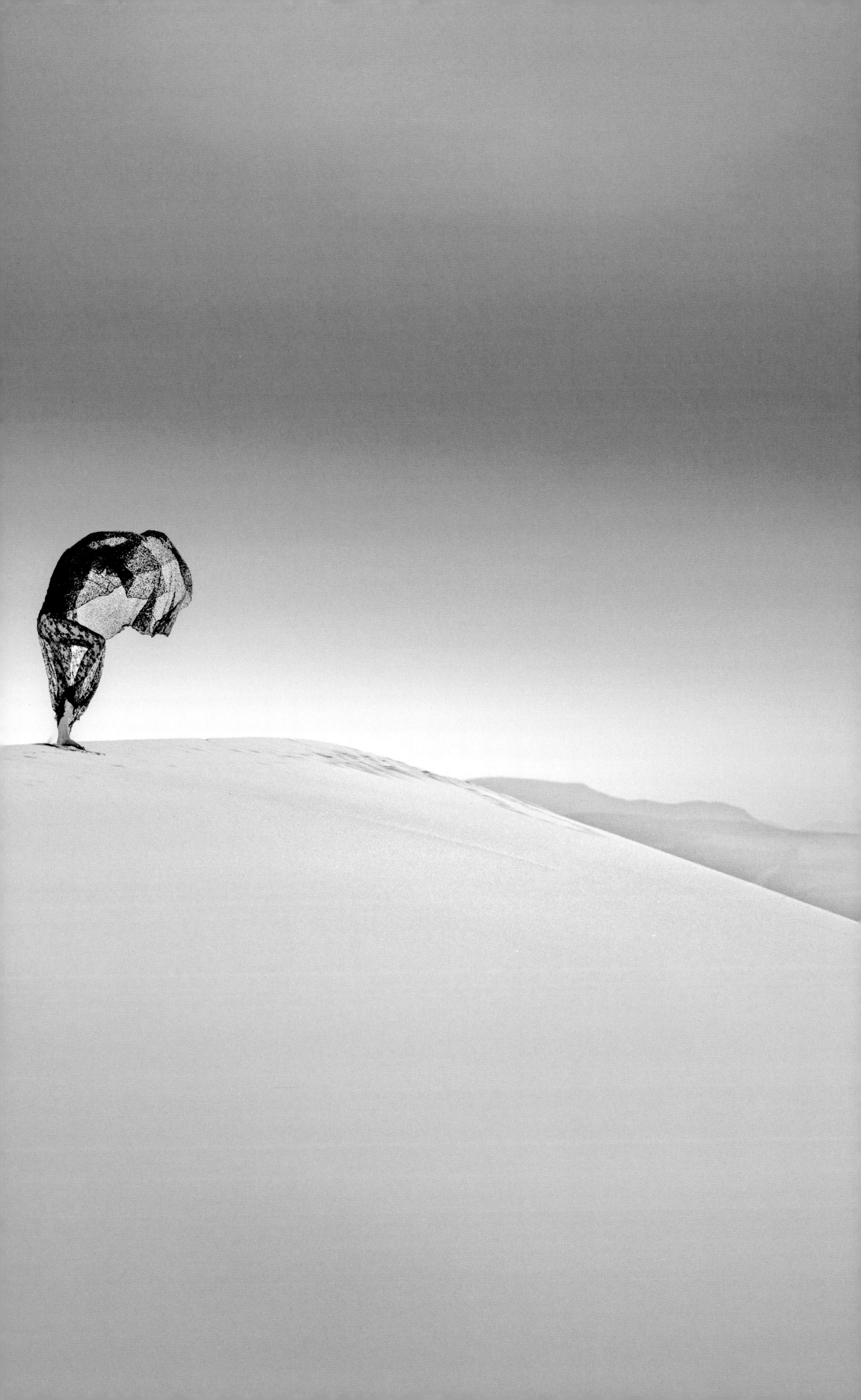

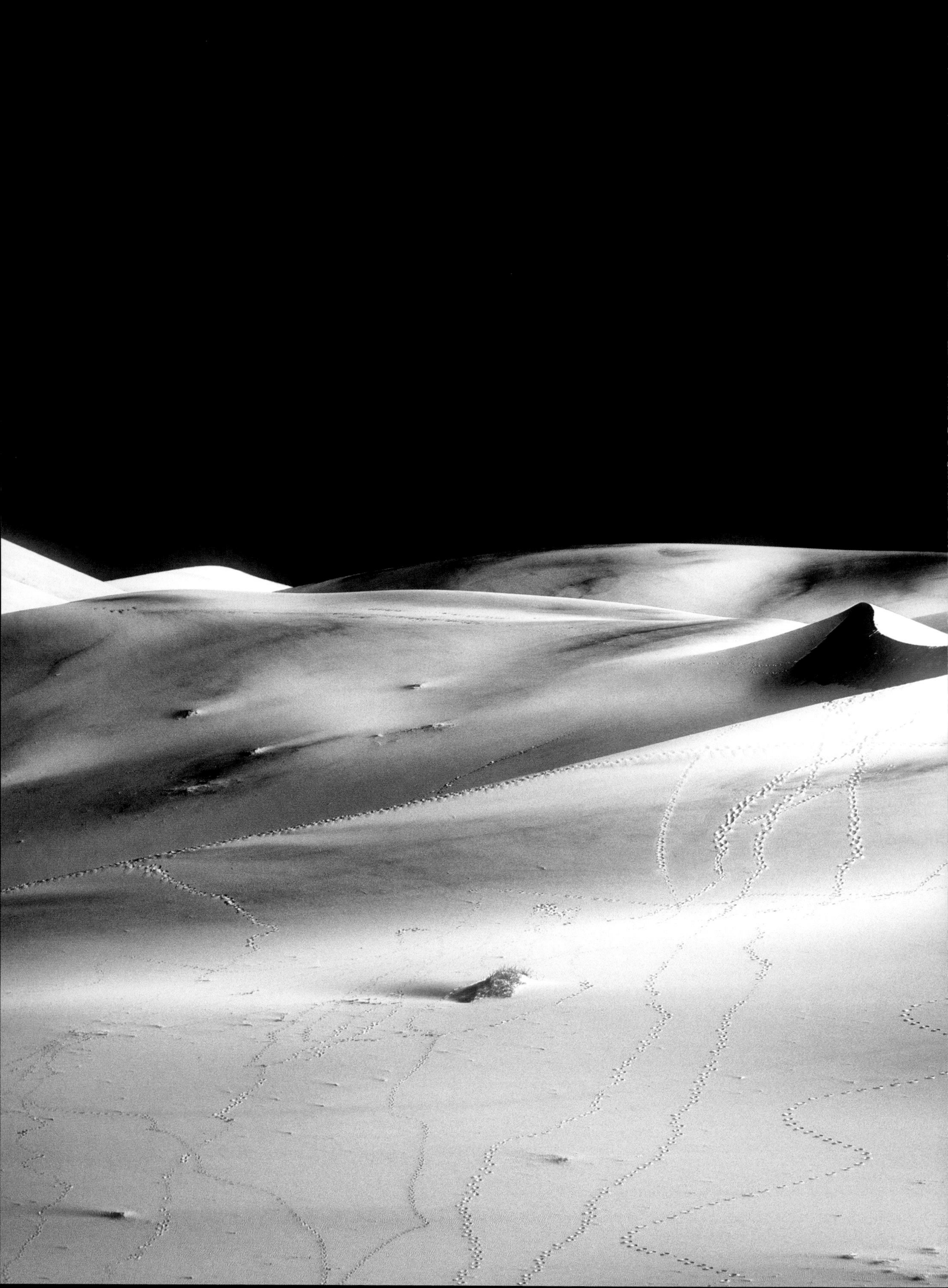

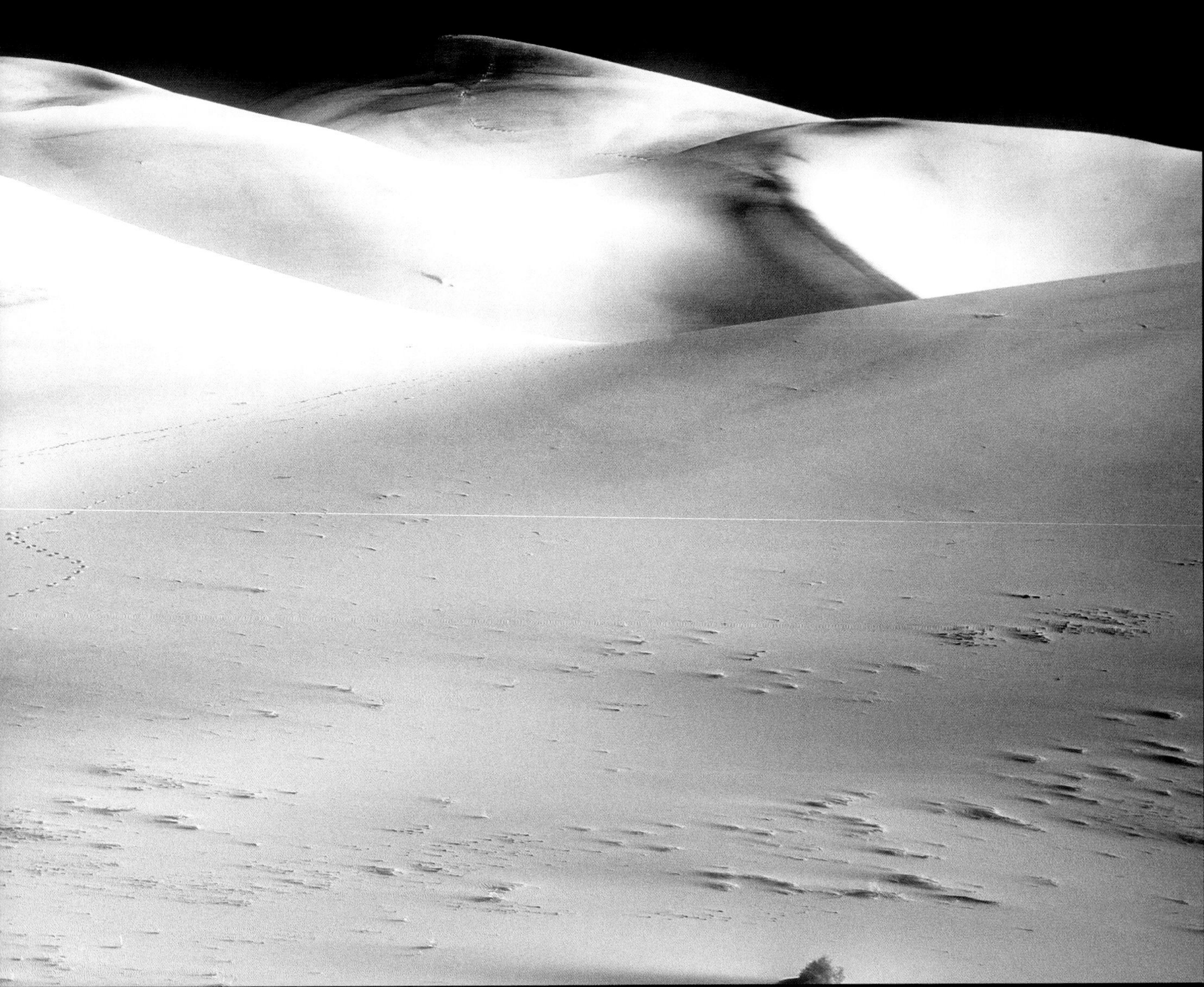

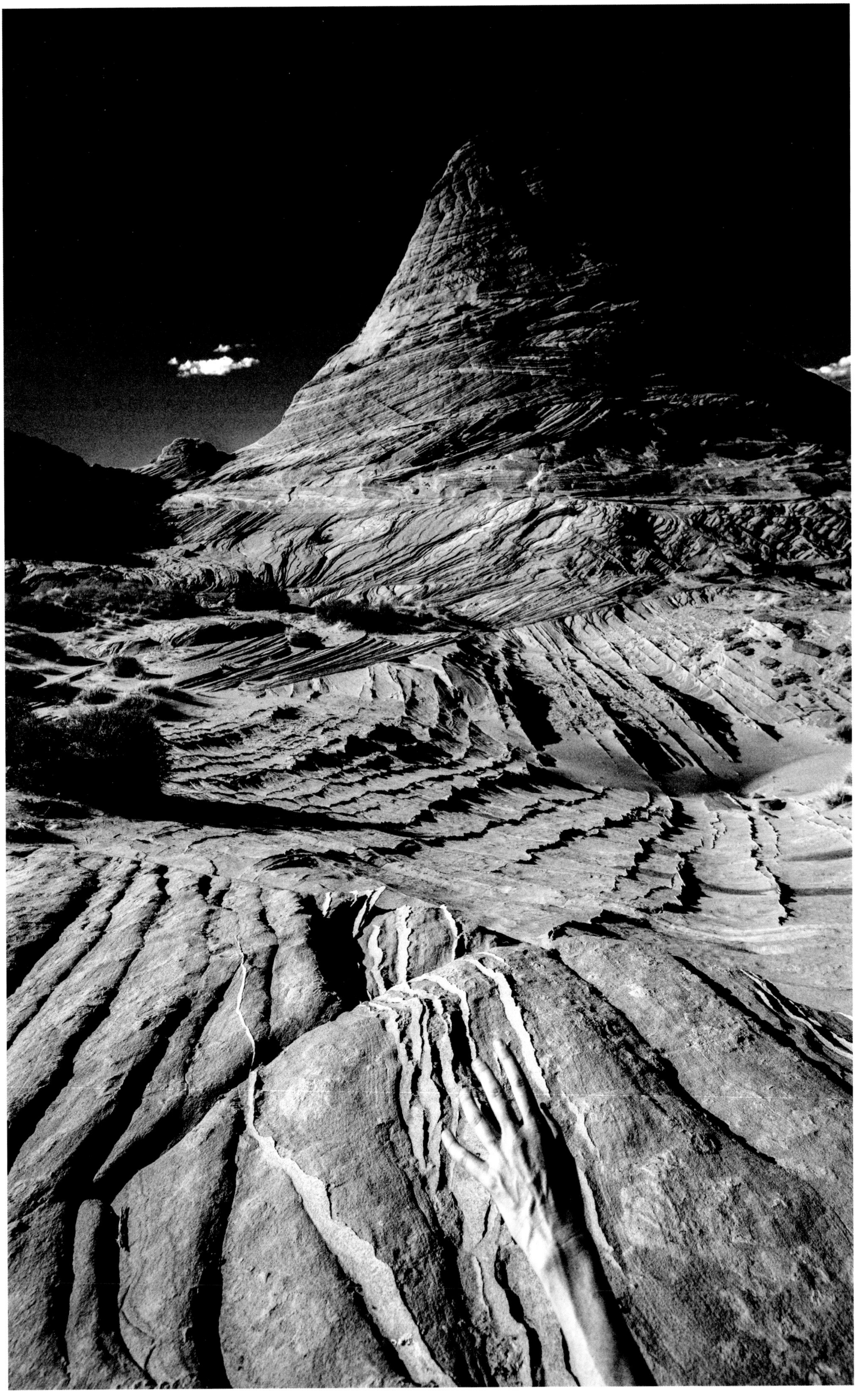

The least of things with a meaning is worth more in life than the greatest of things without it.

—Carl Jung

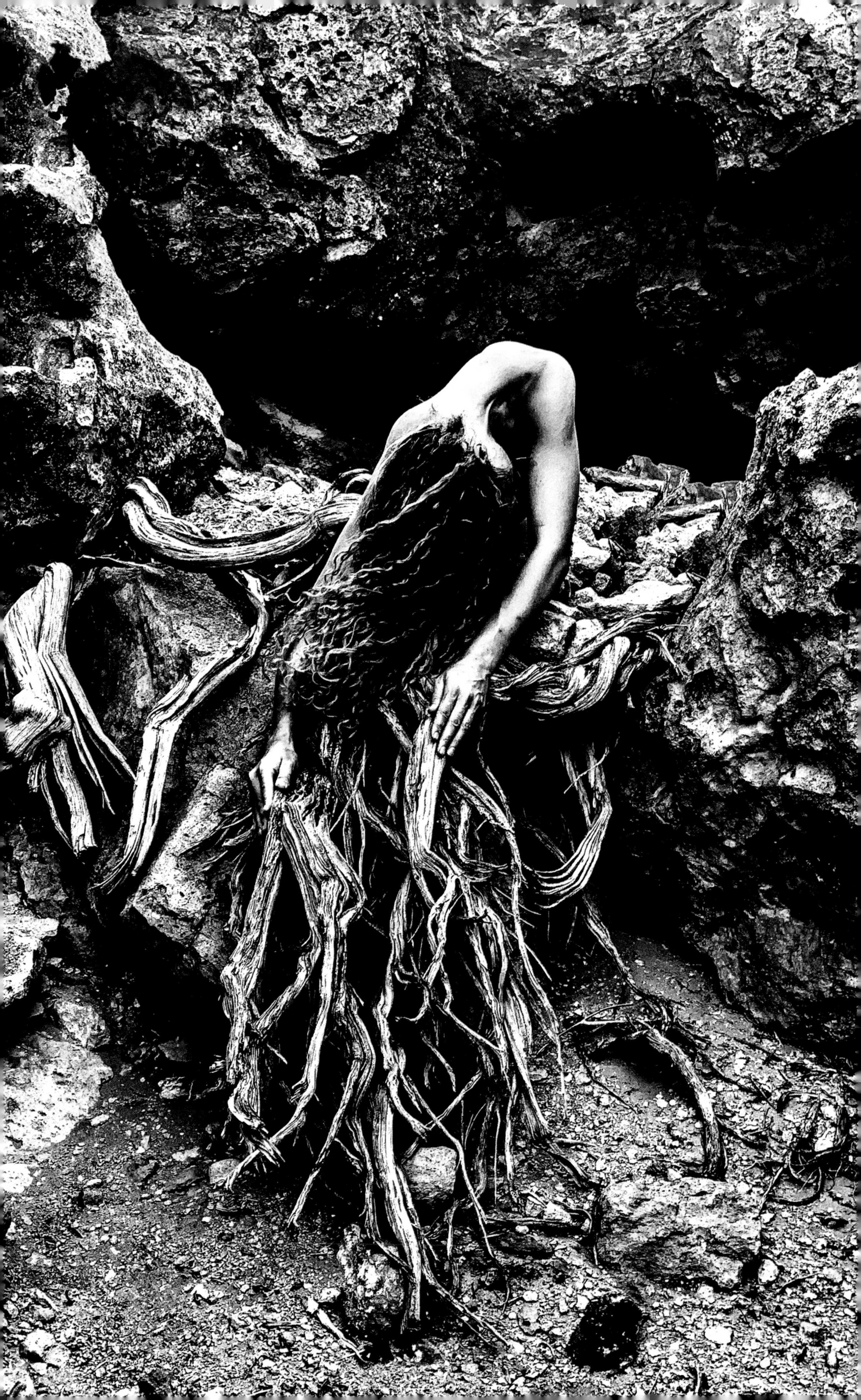

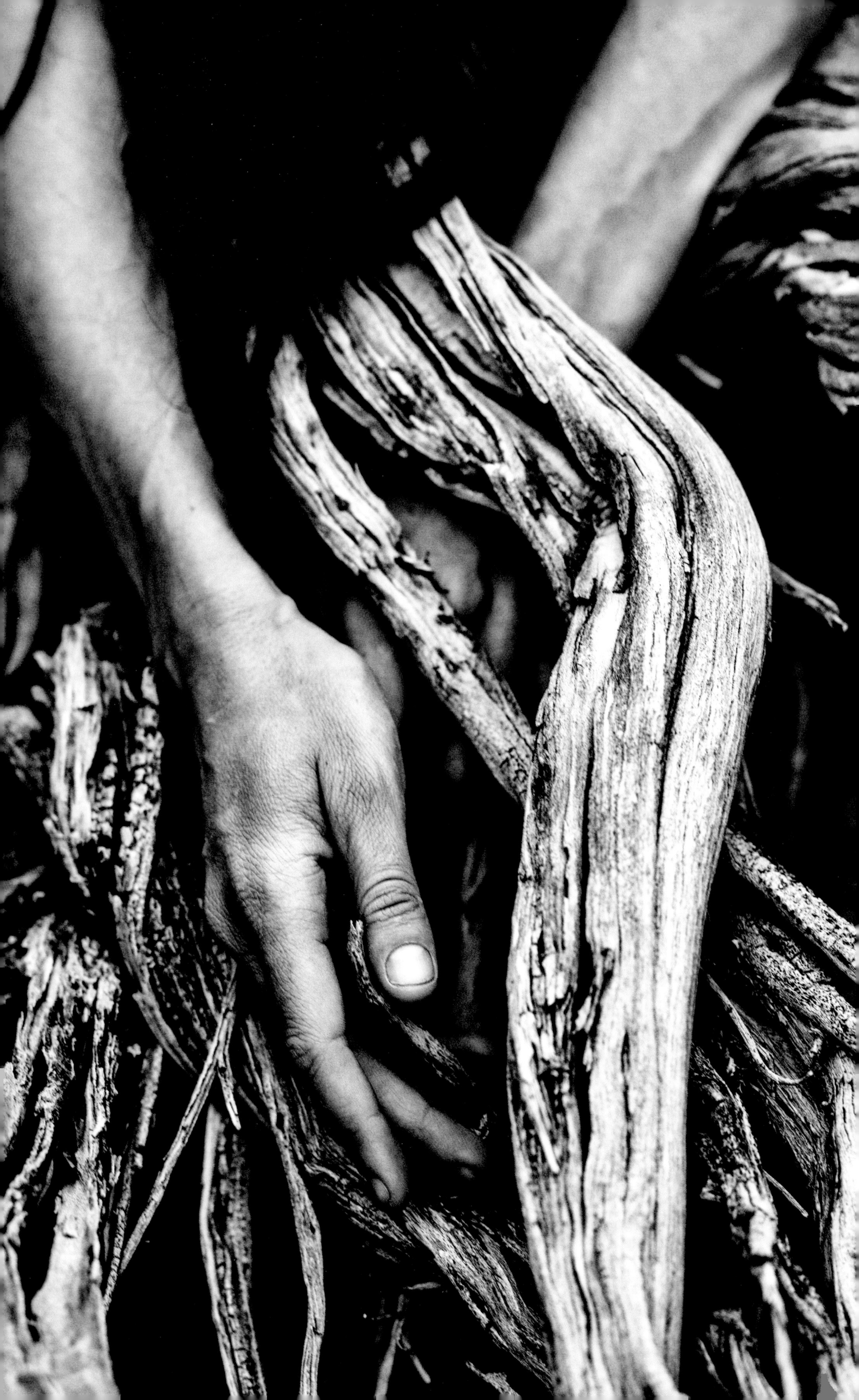

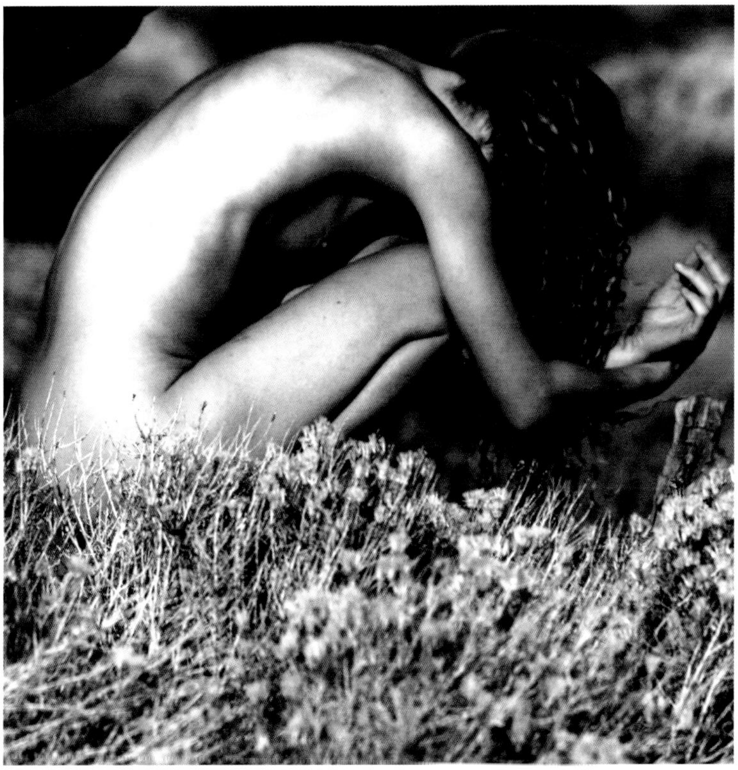

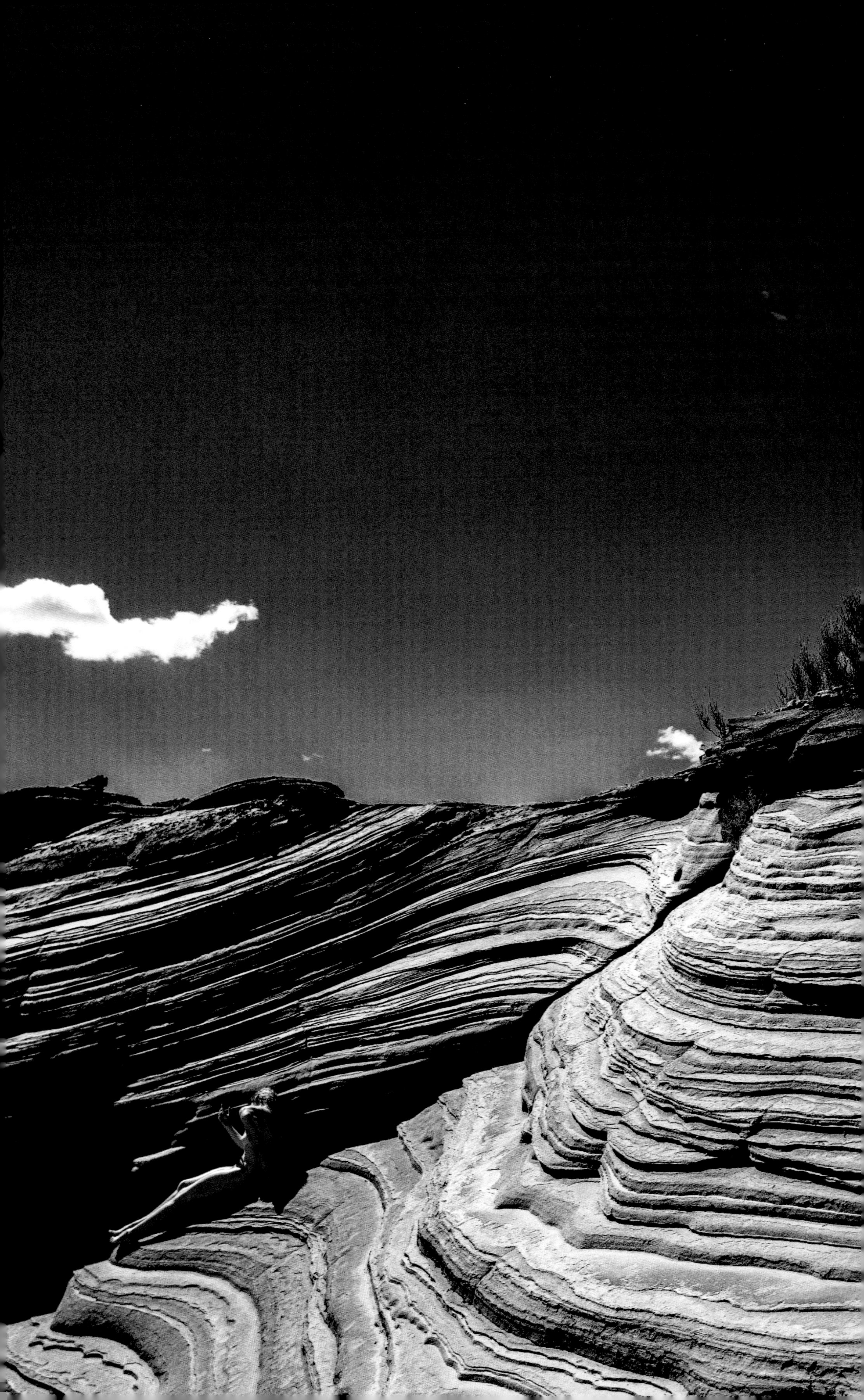

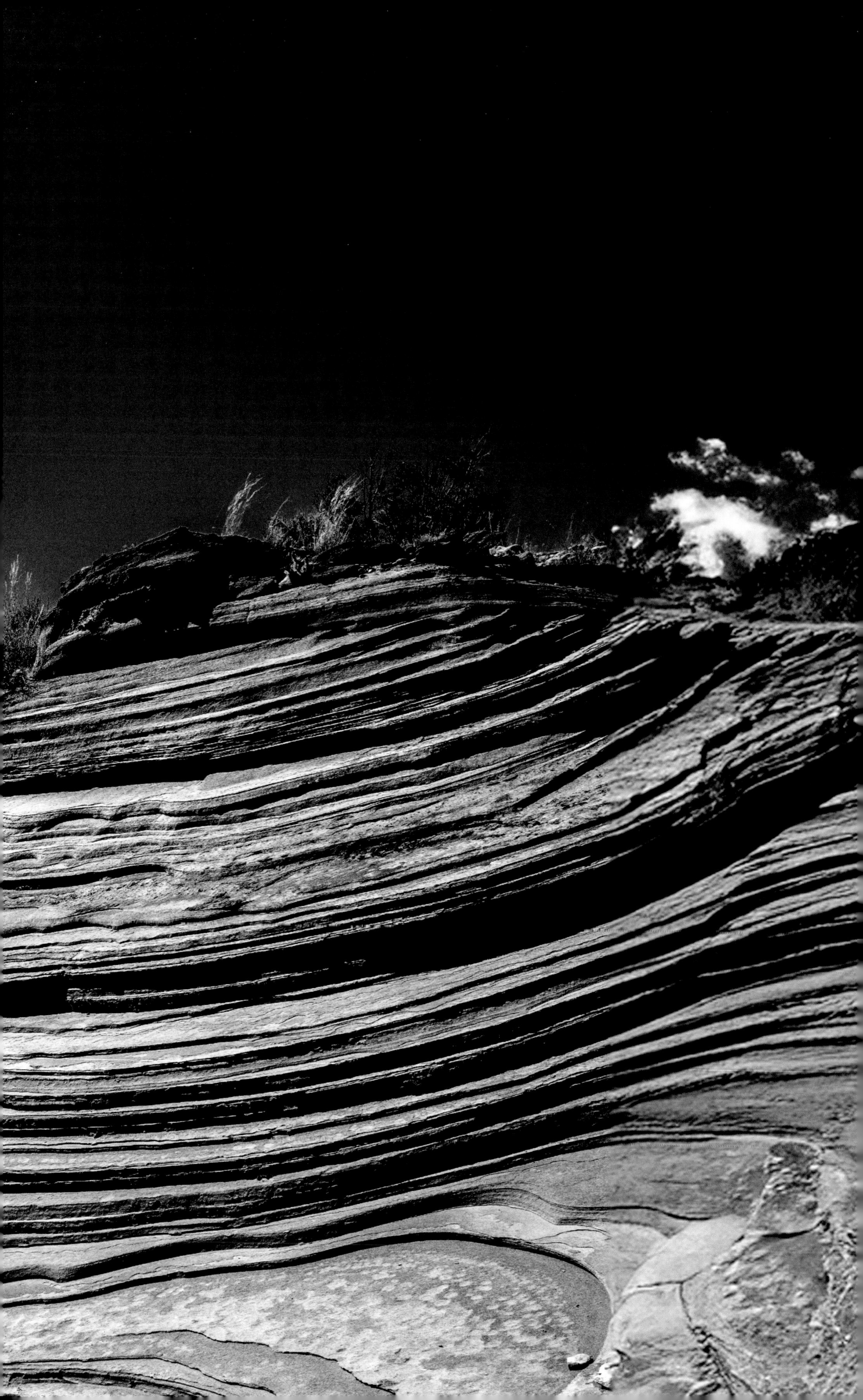

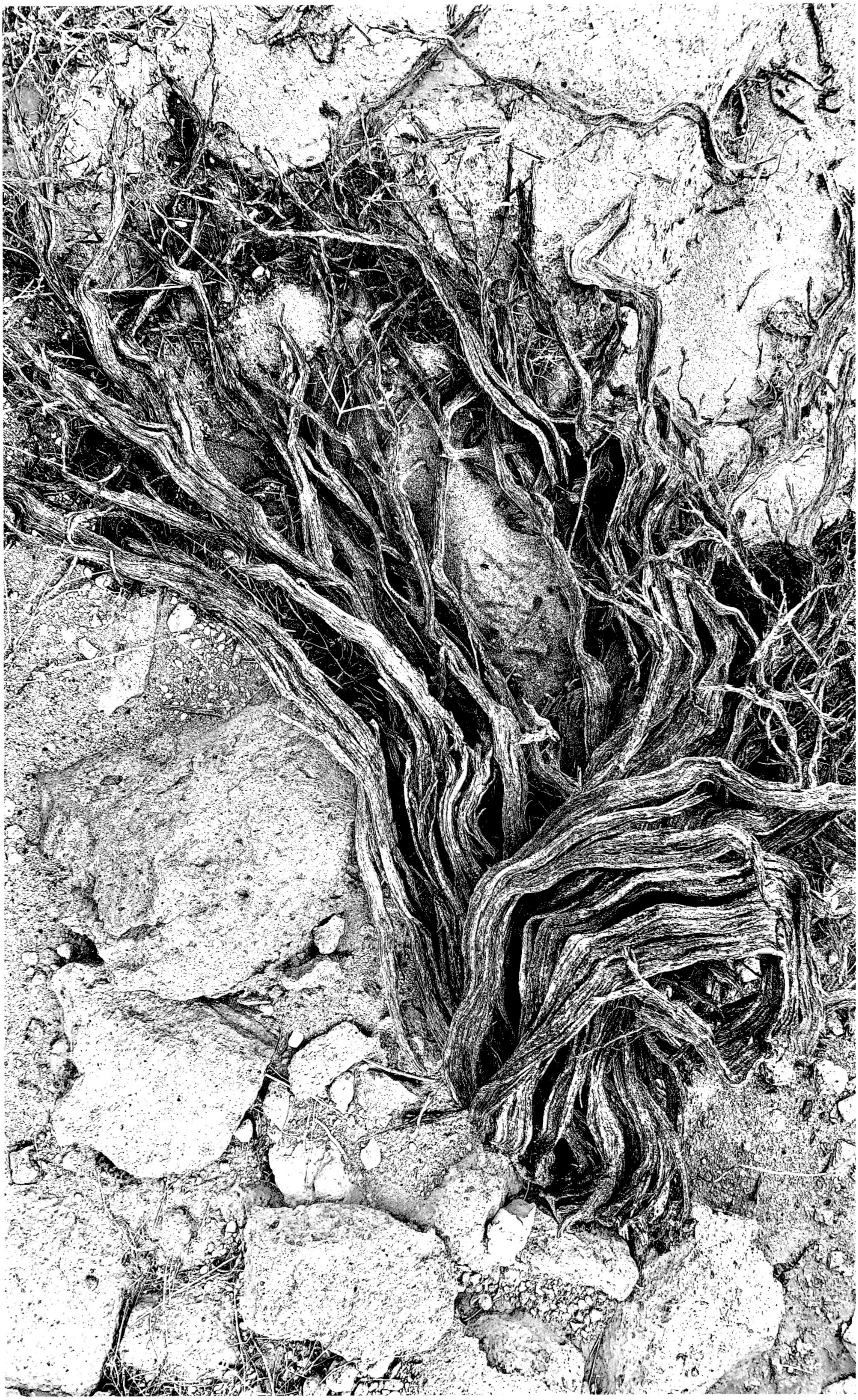

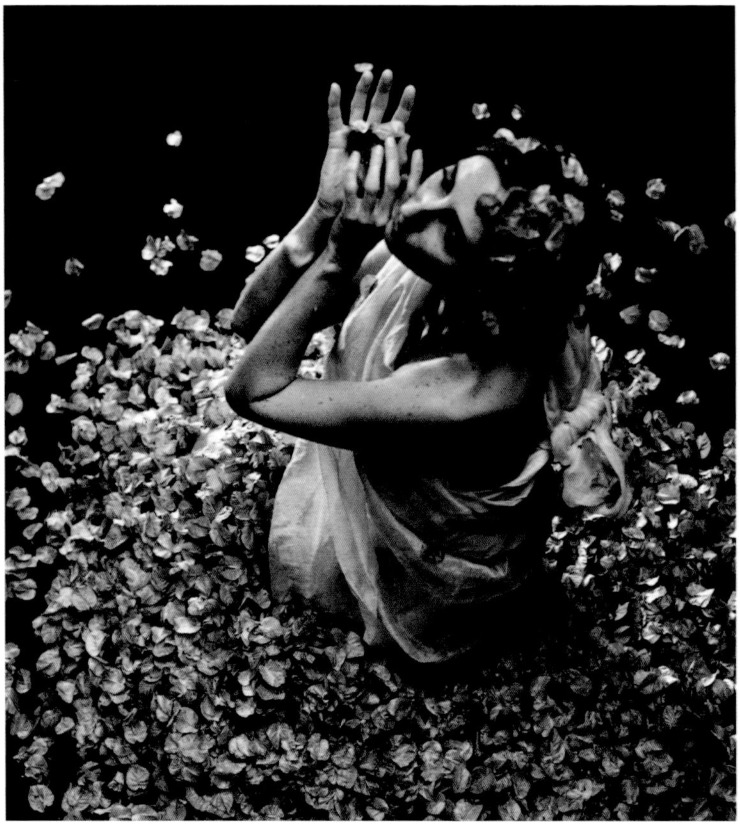

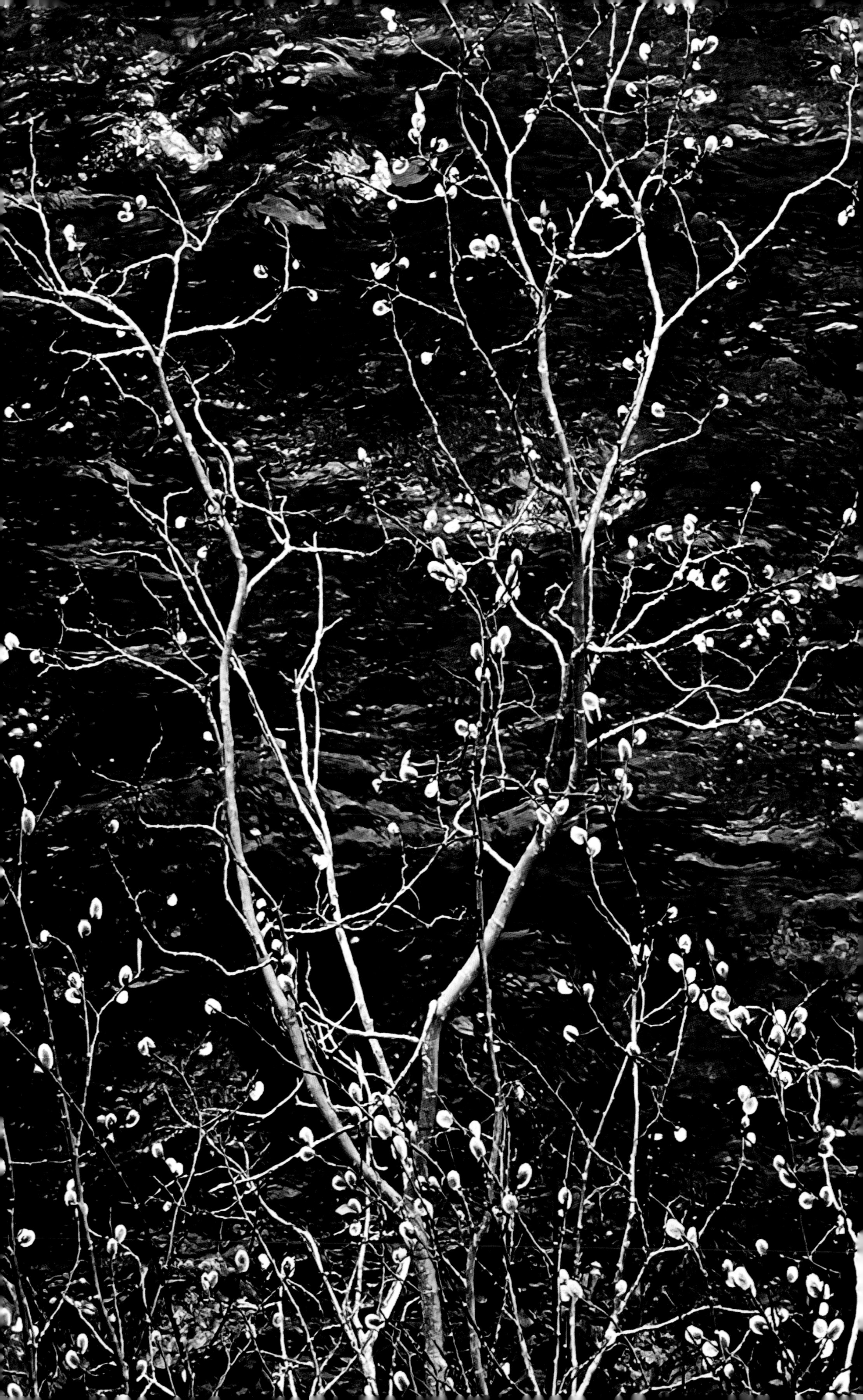

The sea is like music. It has all the dreams of the soul within itself and sounds them over.

—Carl Jung, *Memories, Dreams, Reflections*

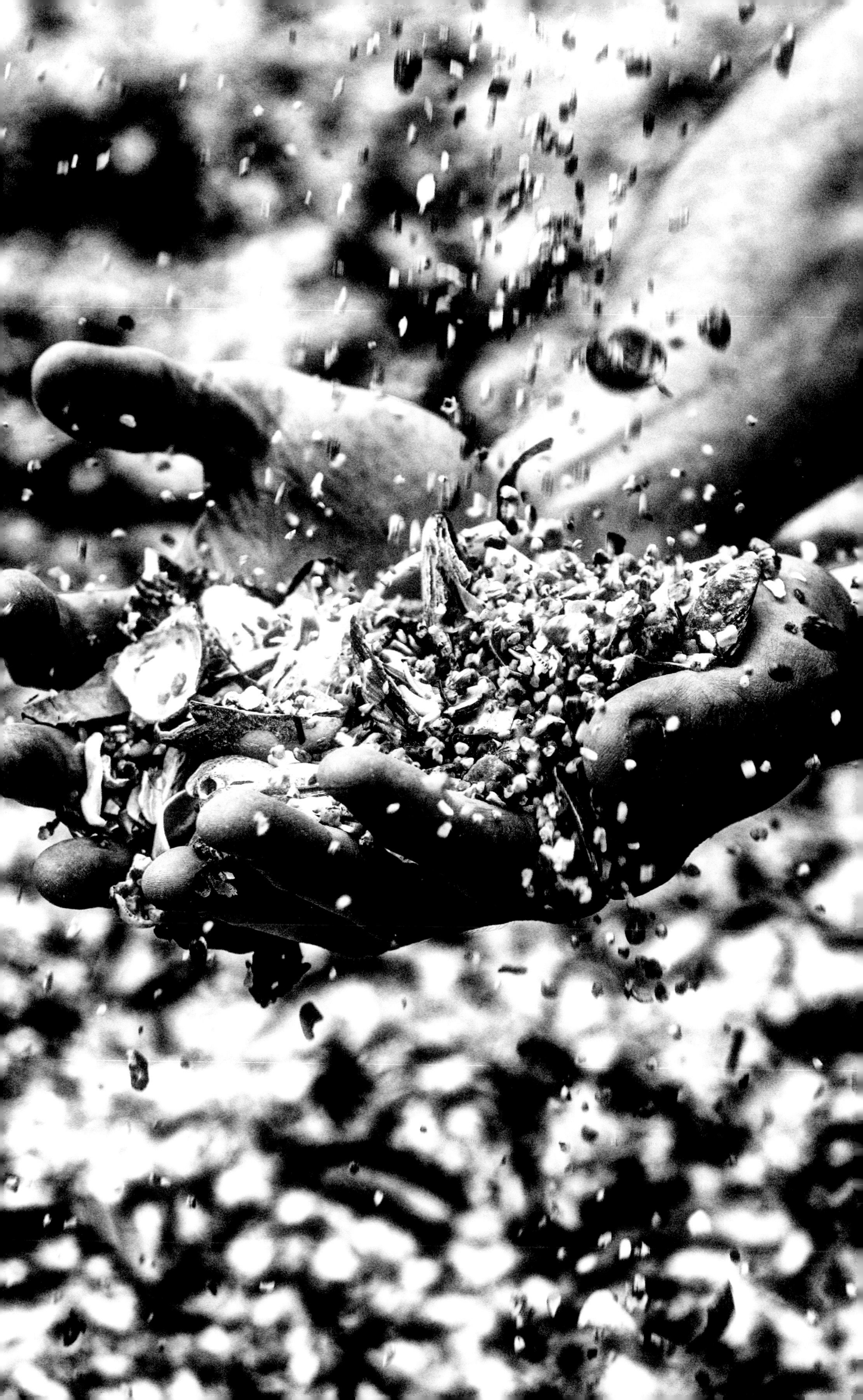

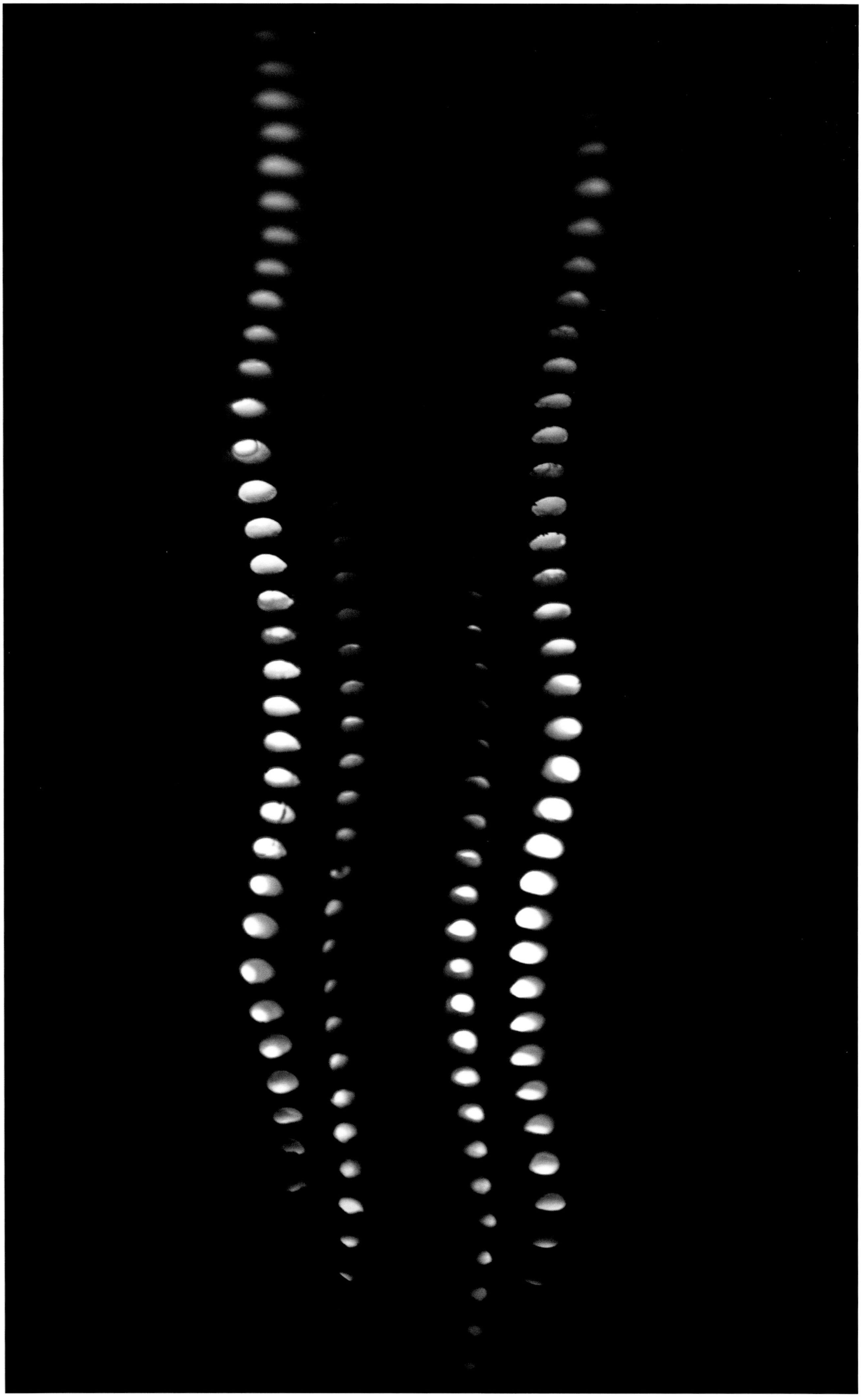

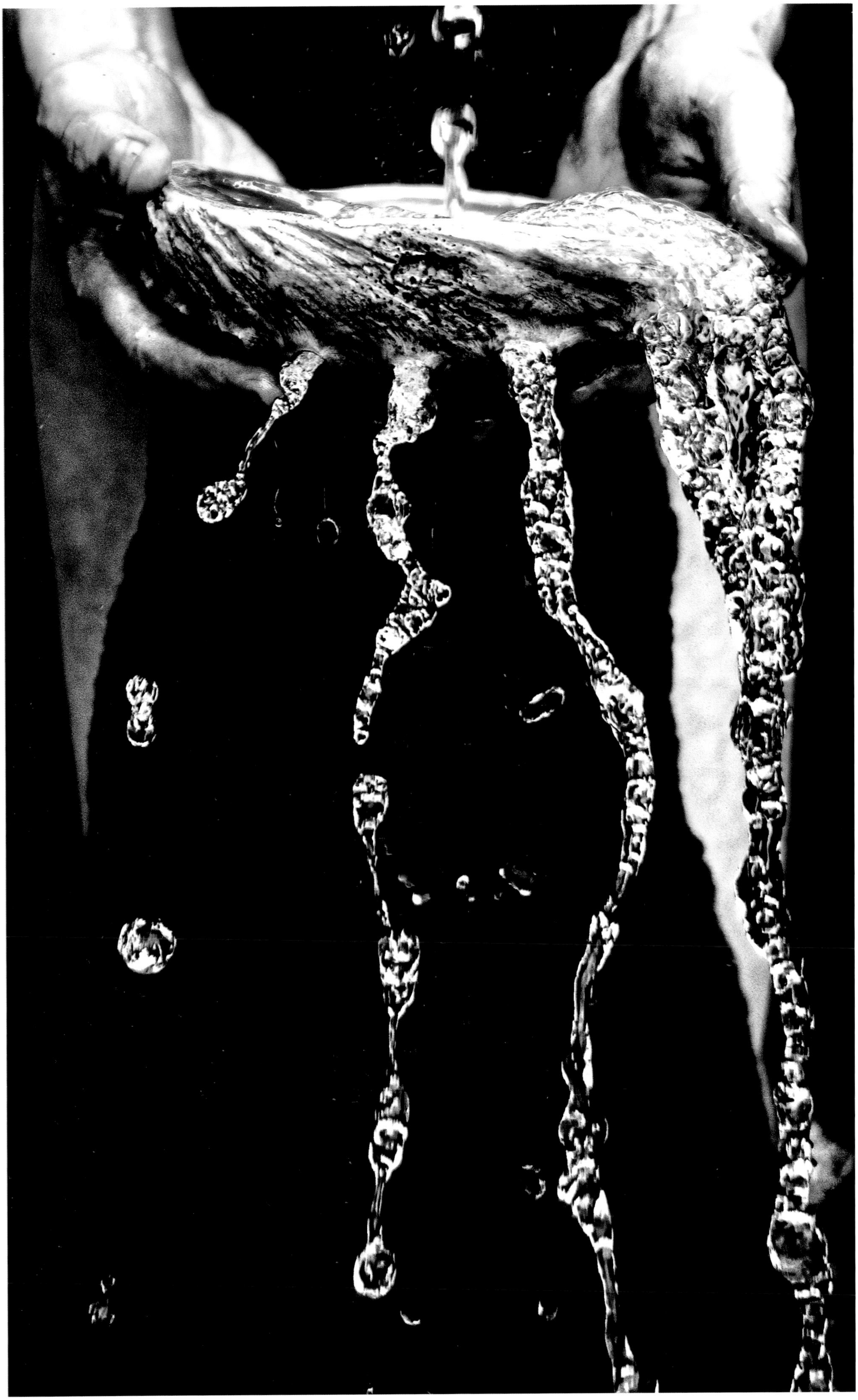

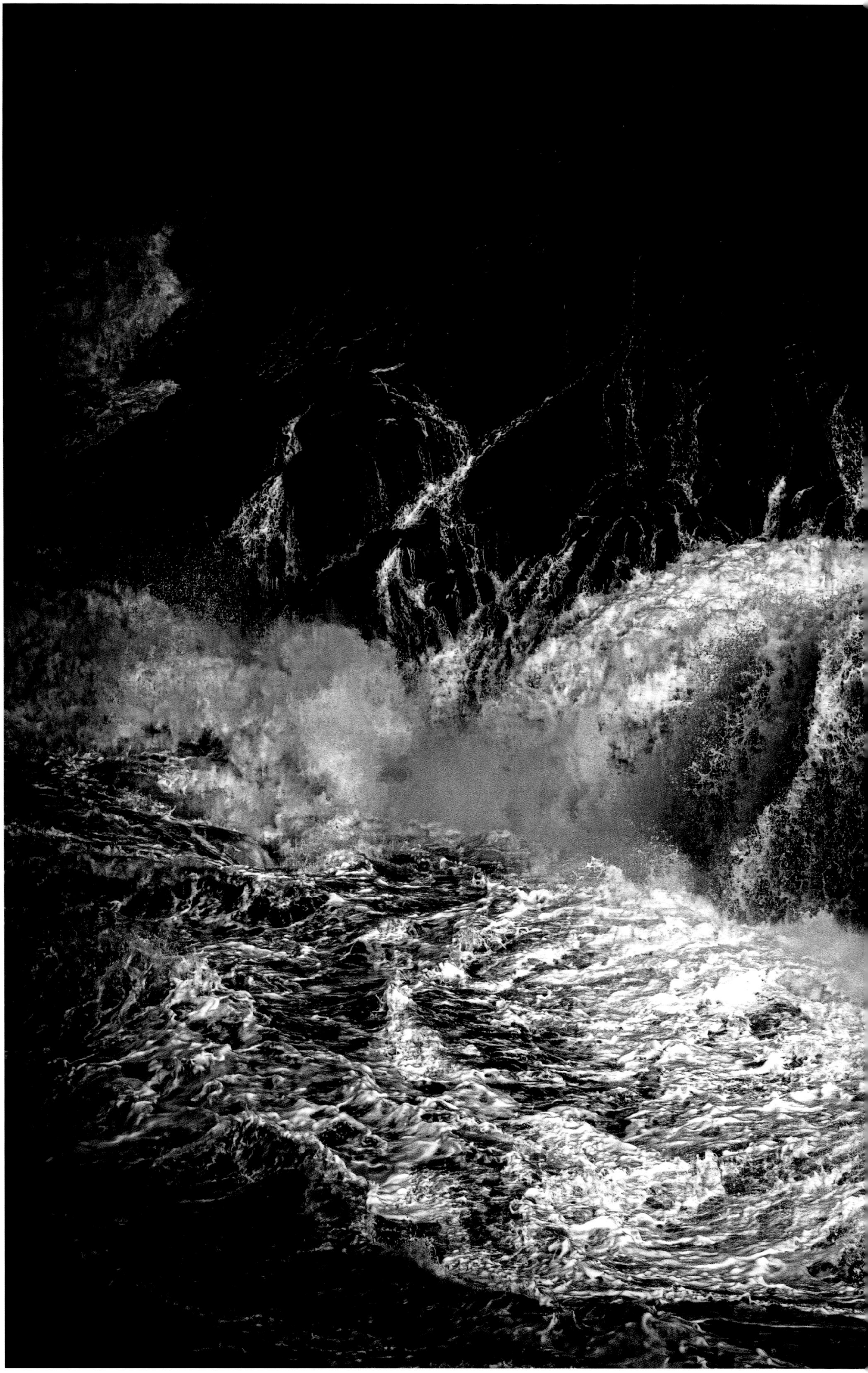

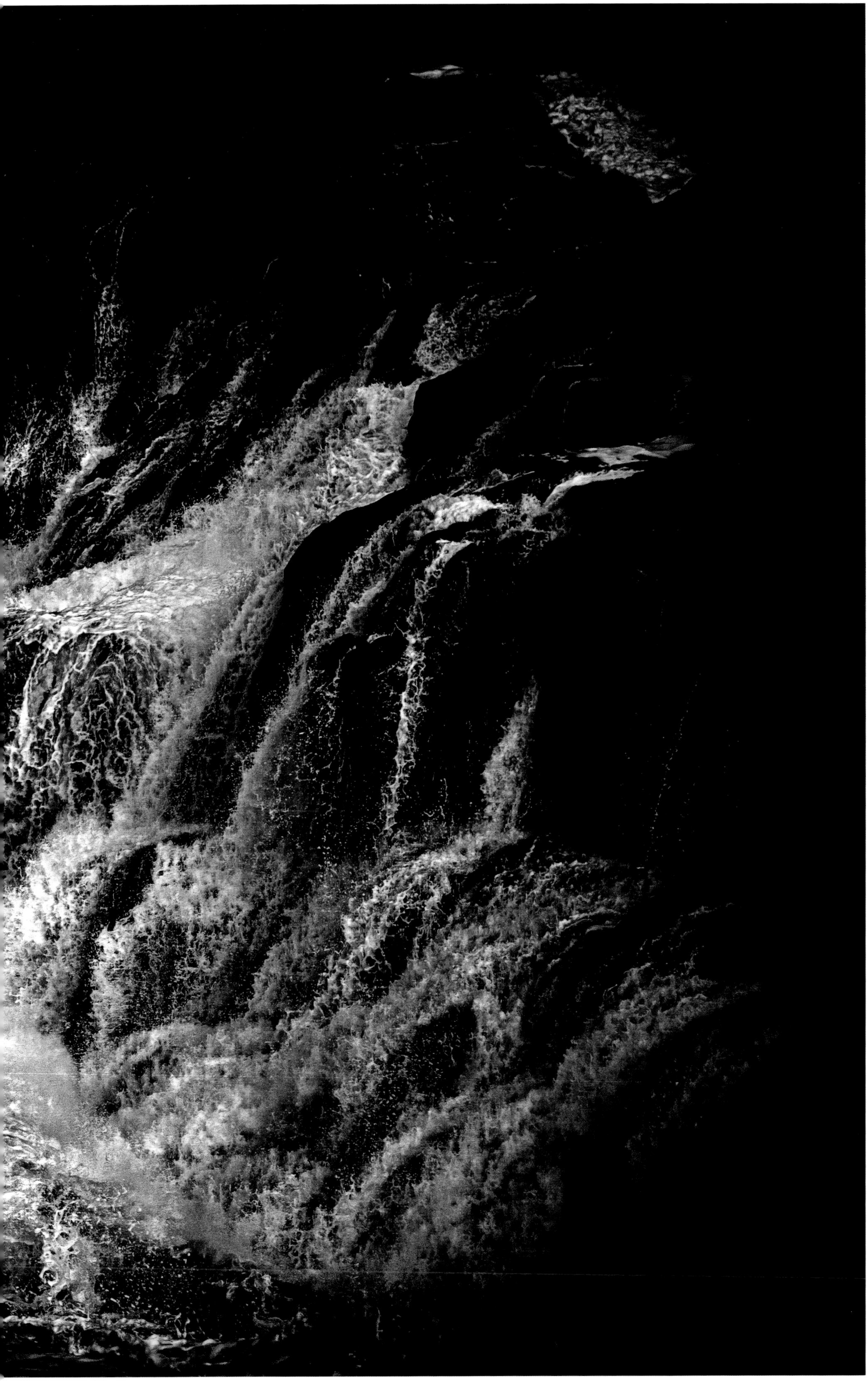

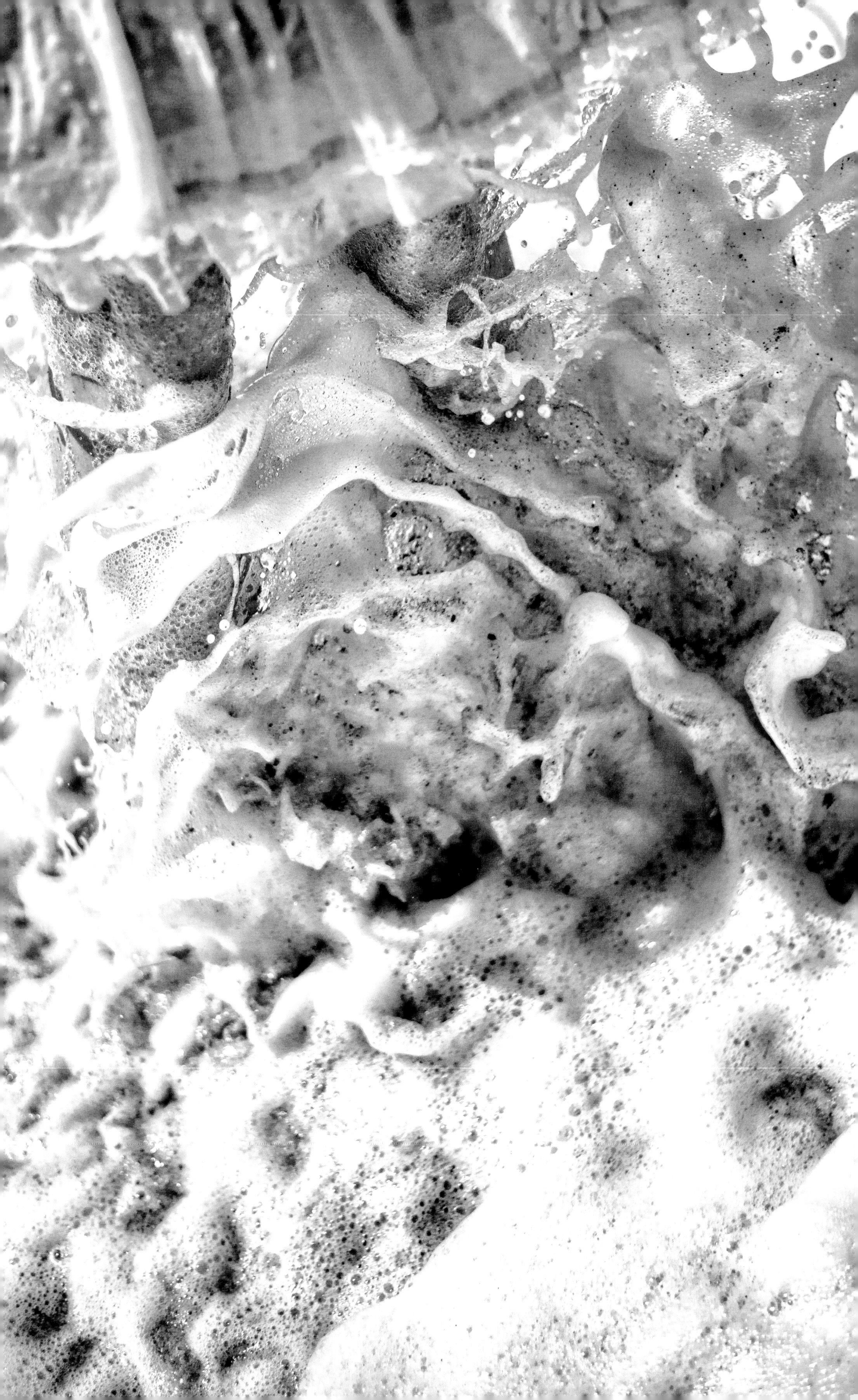

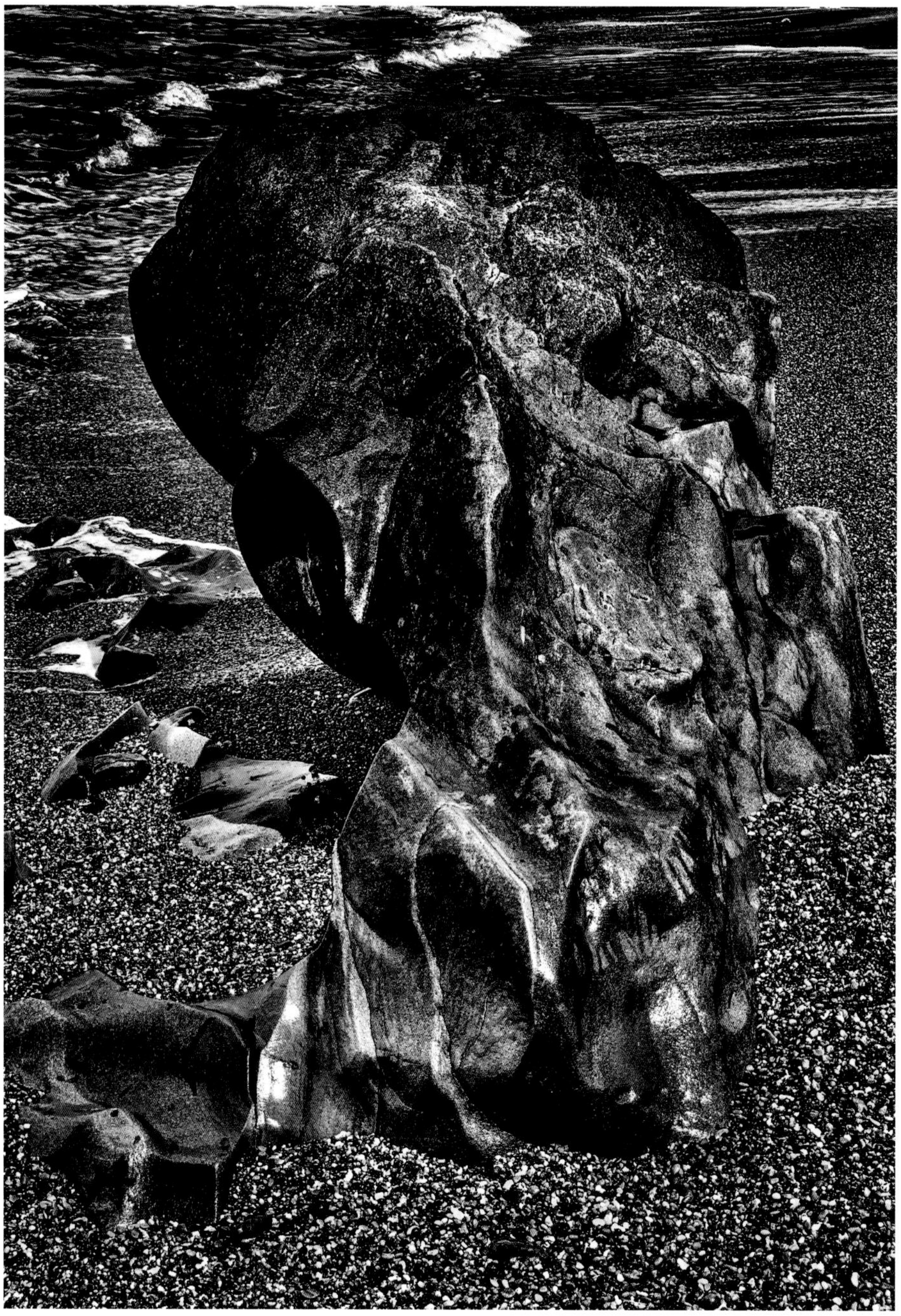

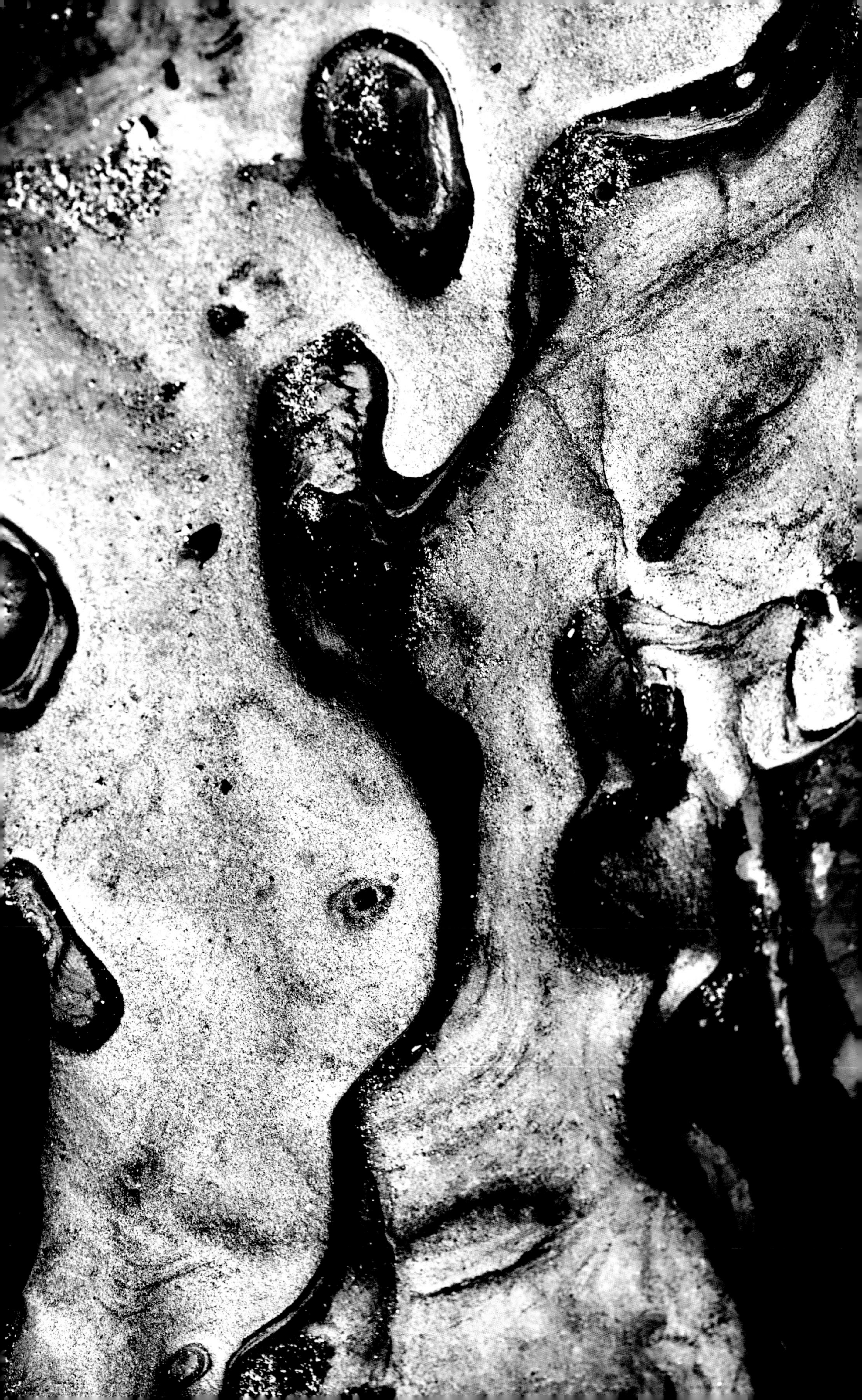

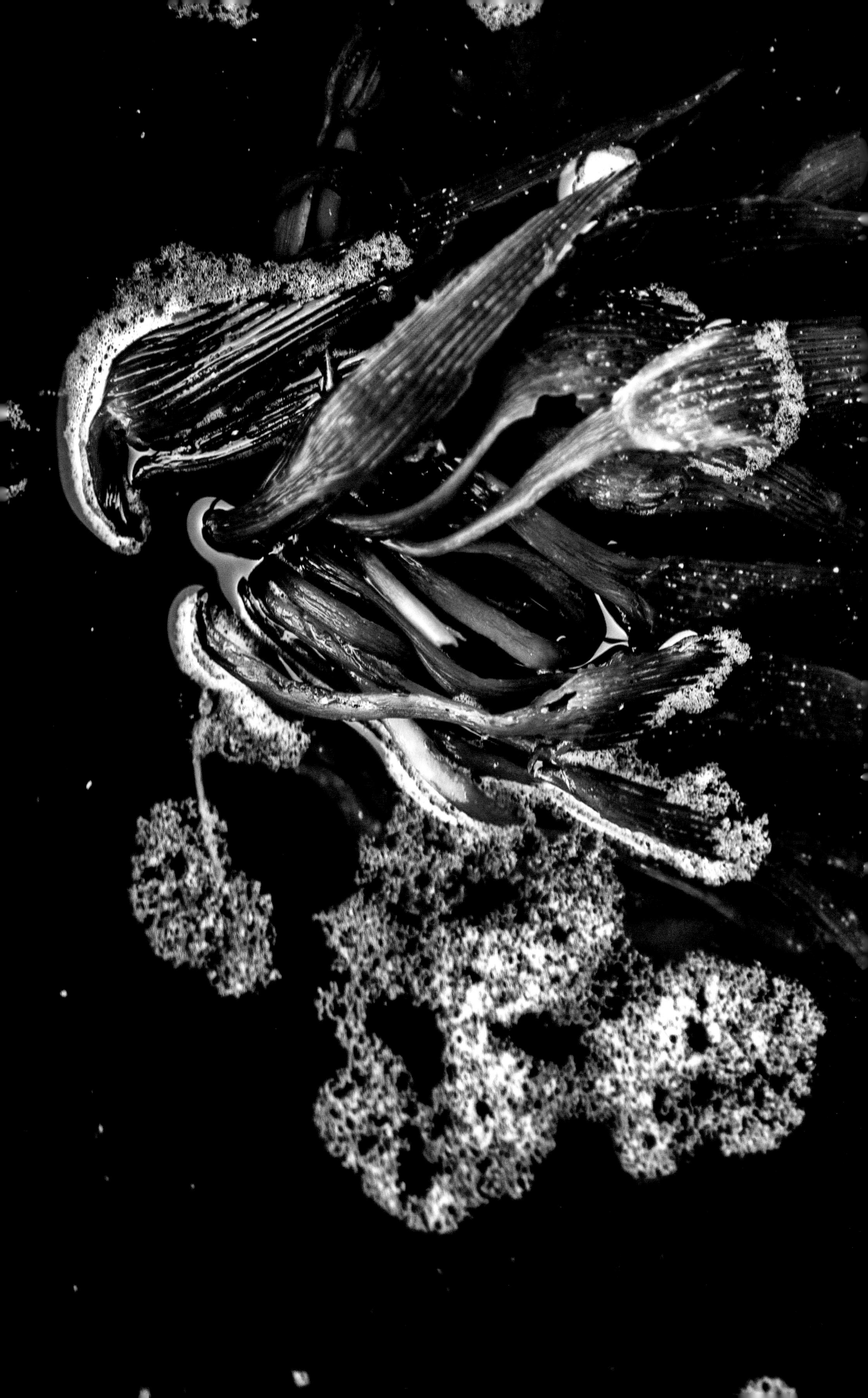

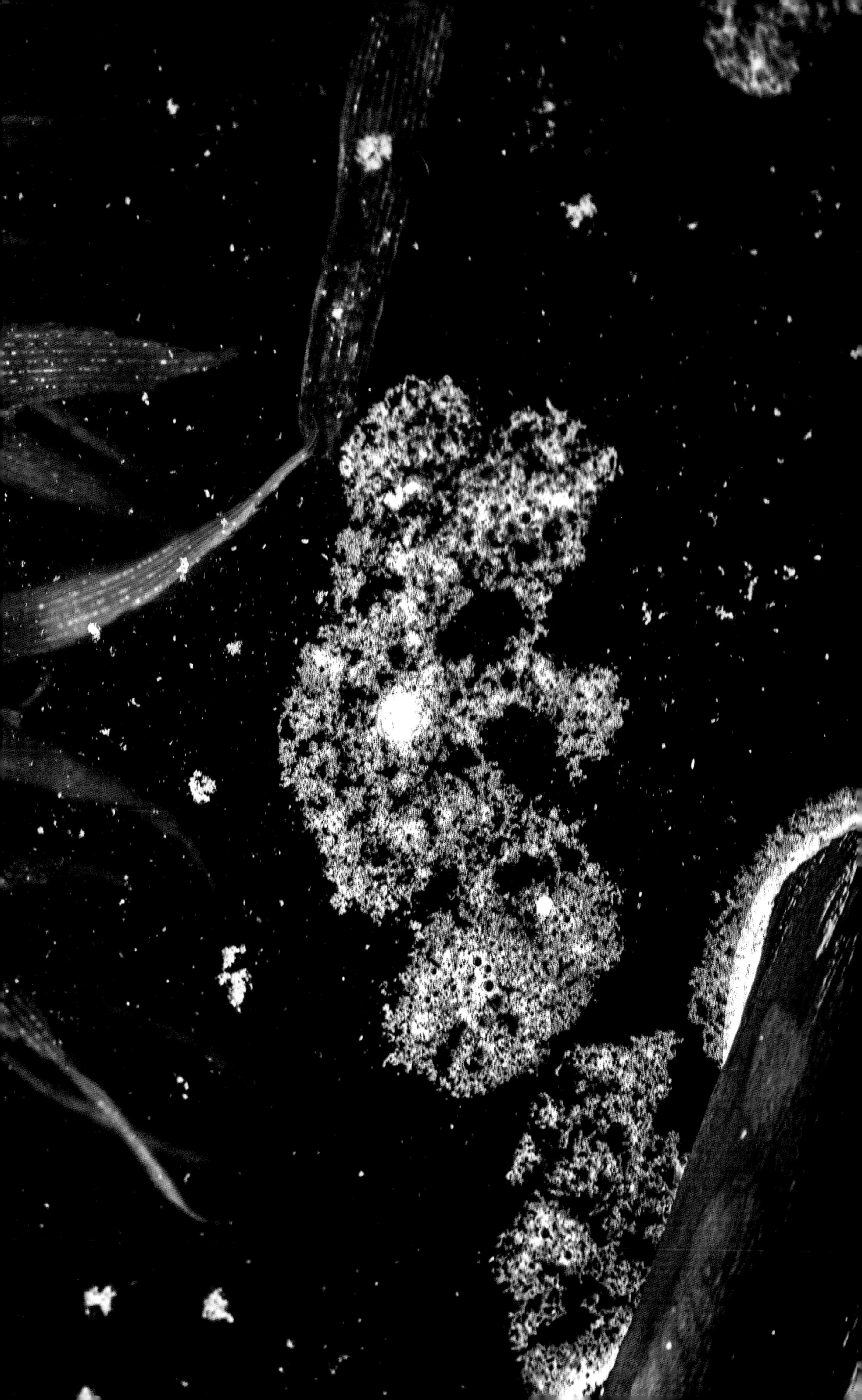

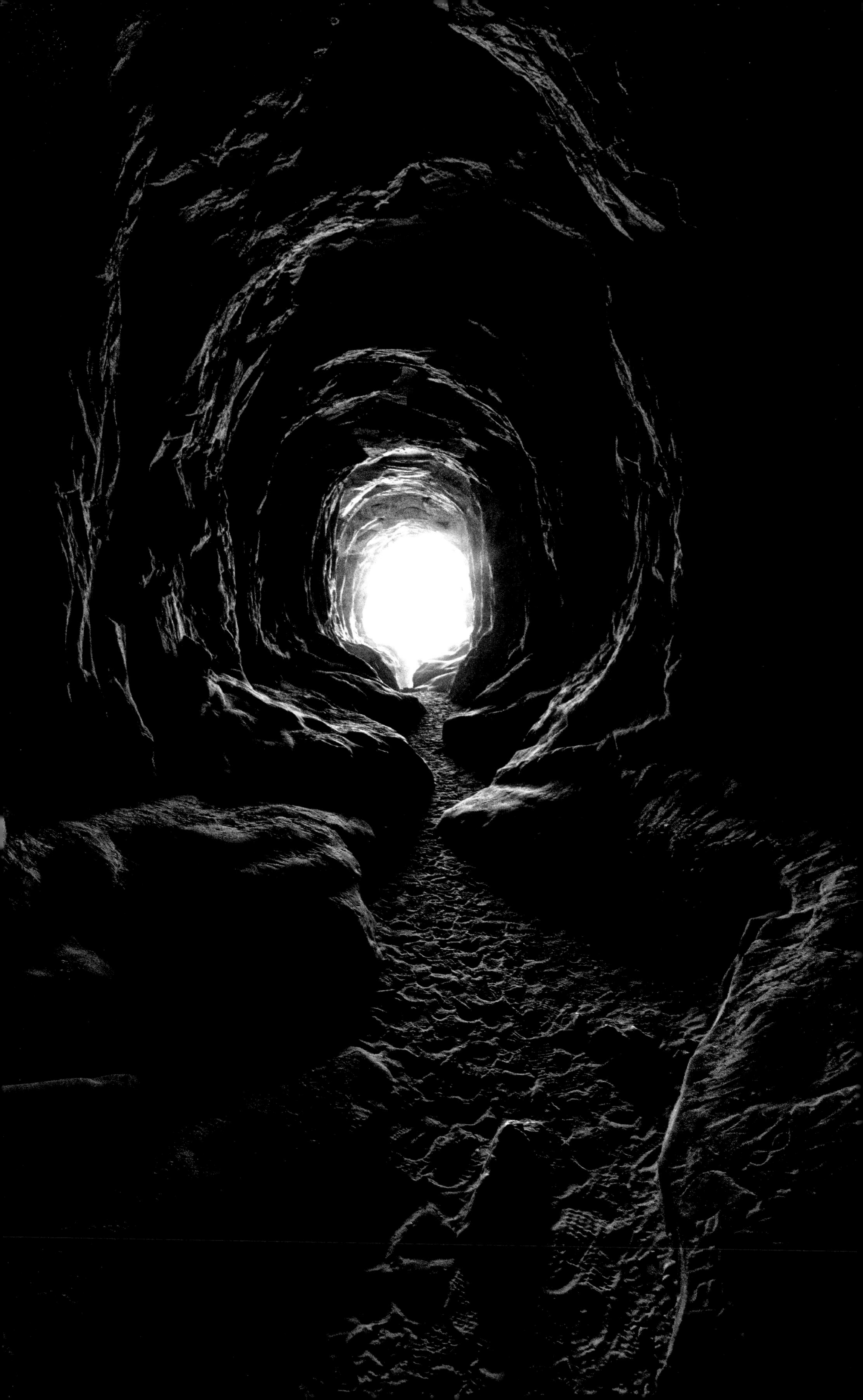

PLATELIST

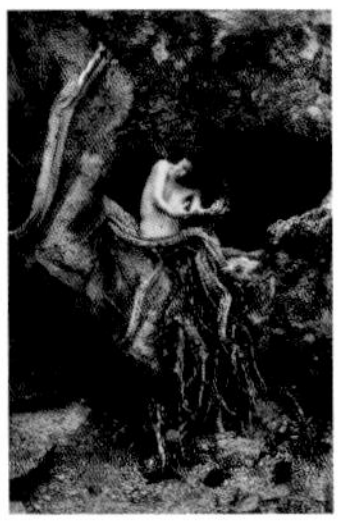
Persephone I

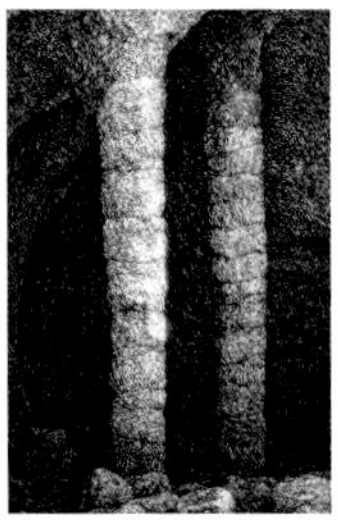
Ascending Lava

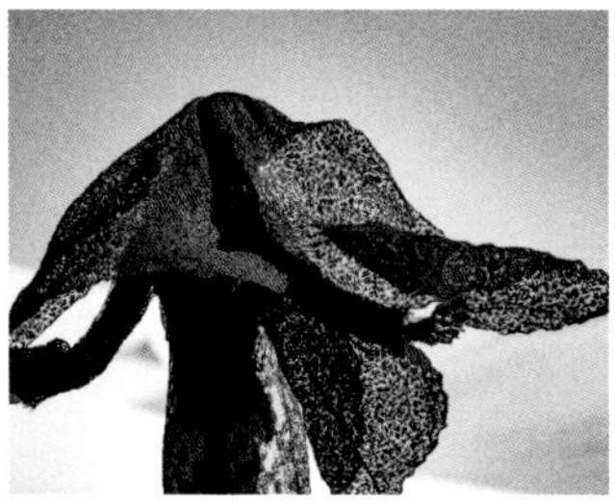
Veiled Truth

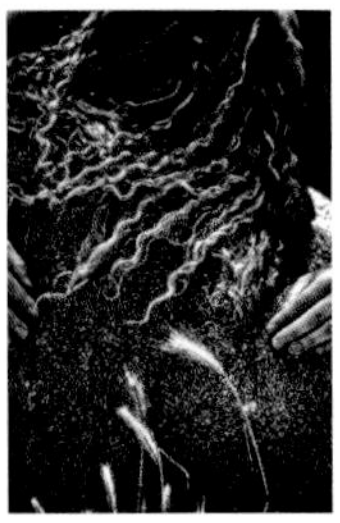
Therian

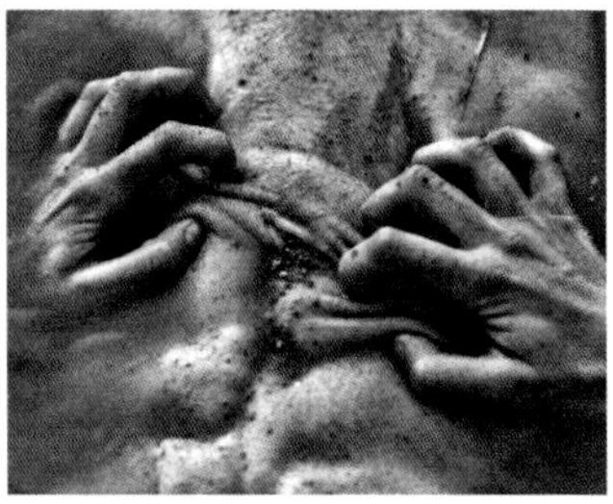
Tumulus

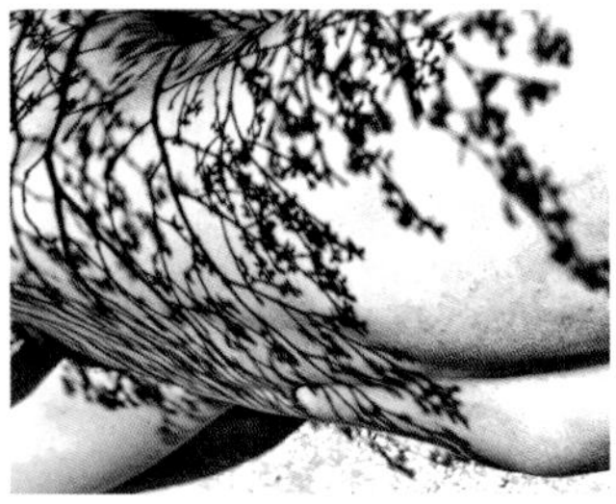
In the Shade of the Rabbit Bush

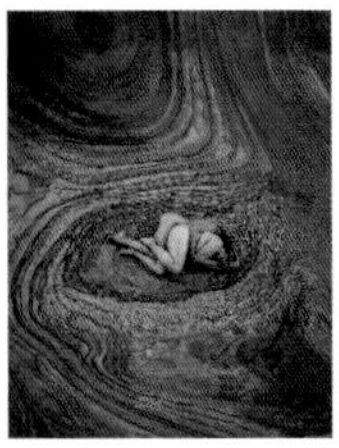
Senescence

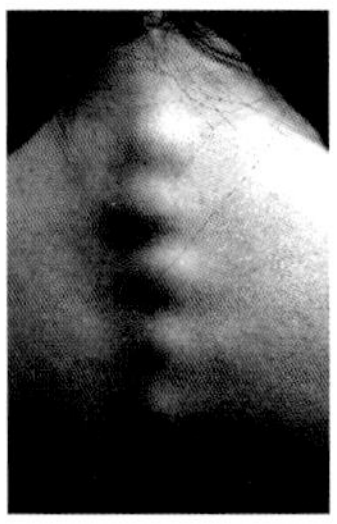
Sweet Umi

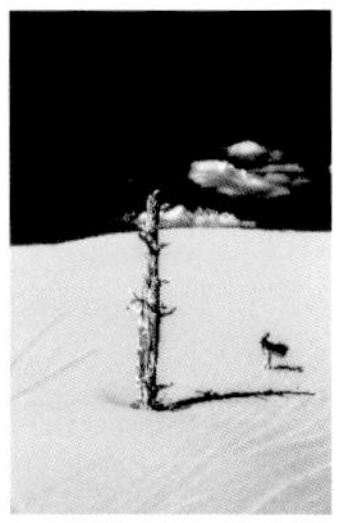
Totem

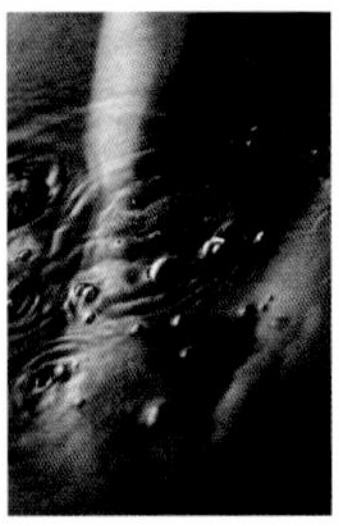
Descend

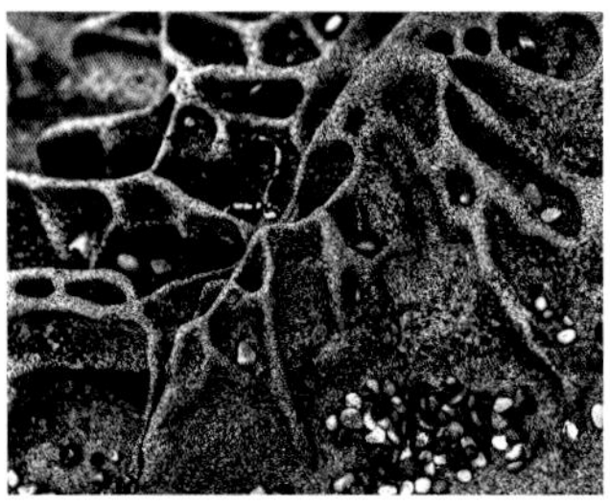
Circulation

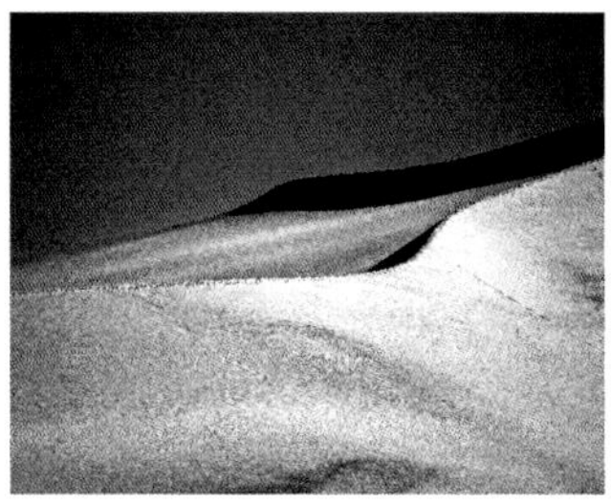
Spine

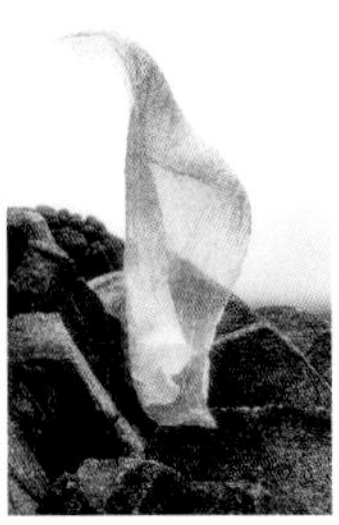
Veil

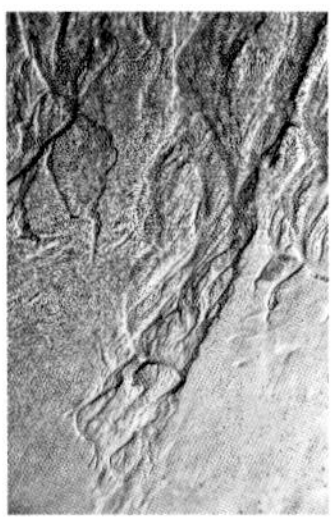
Ebbing

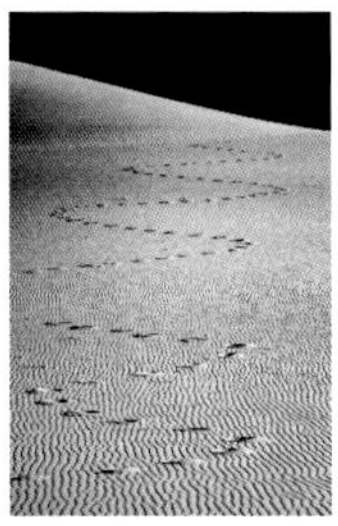
Infinity

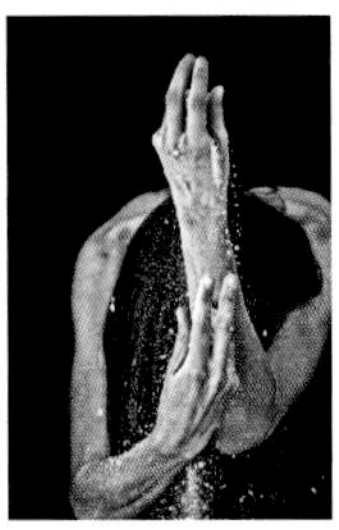
Falling Ash

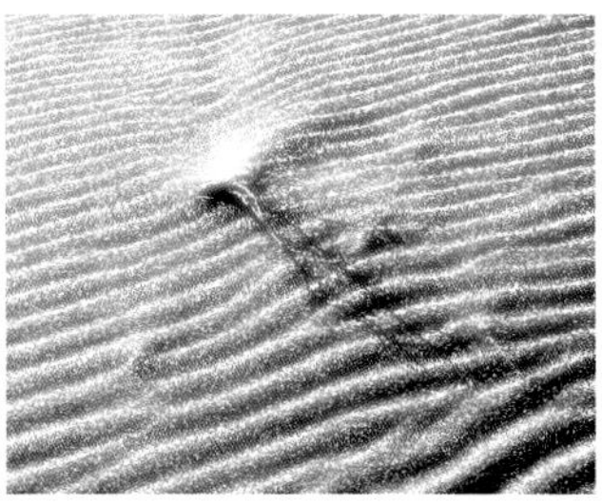
Solar Waves

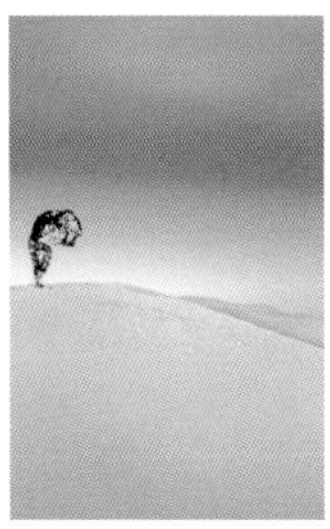
Kokopelli

Argent

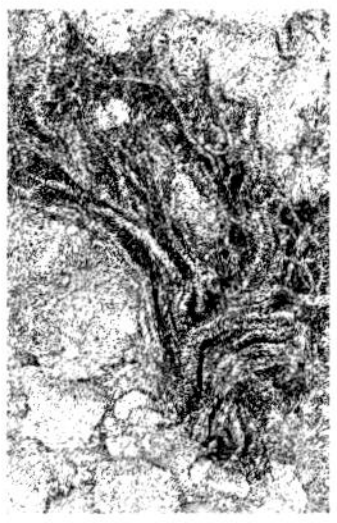
Past Life

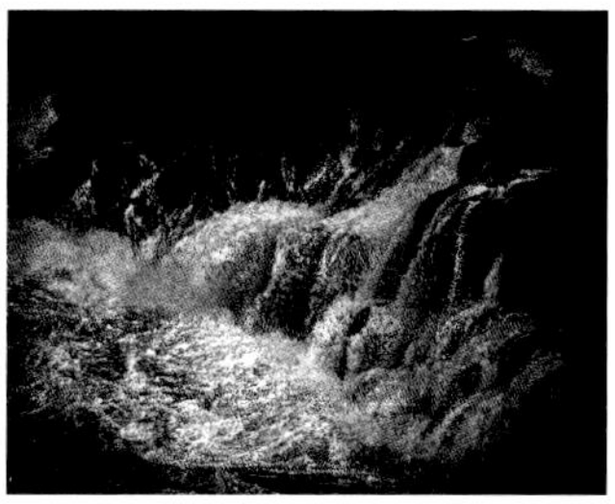
Fiery

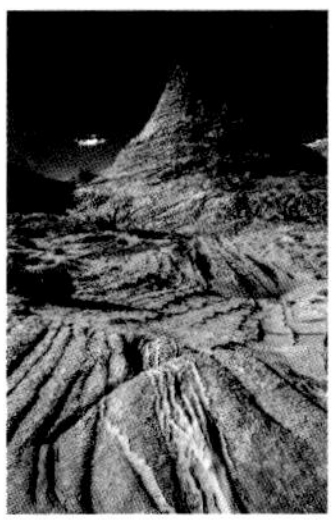
Hive

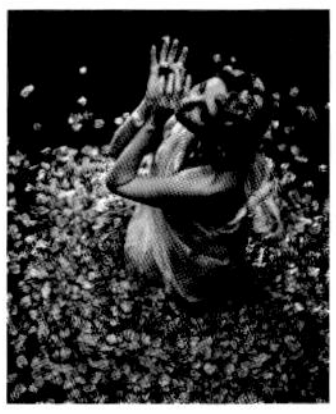
Anointed

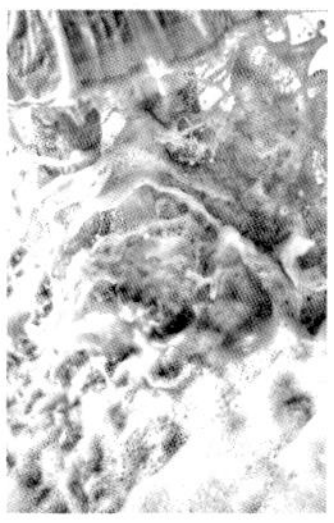
Tidal Zone

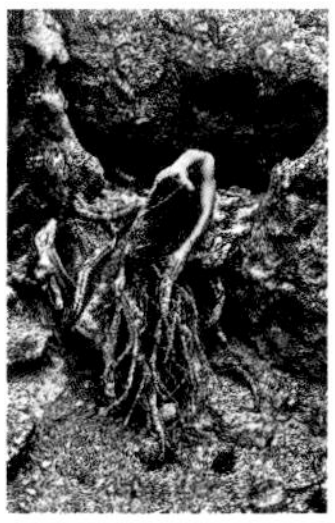
Persephone II

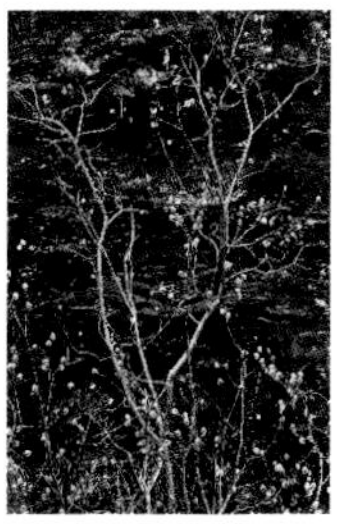
Willow

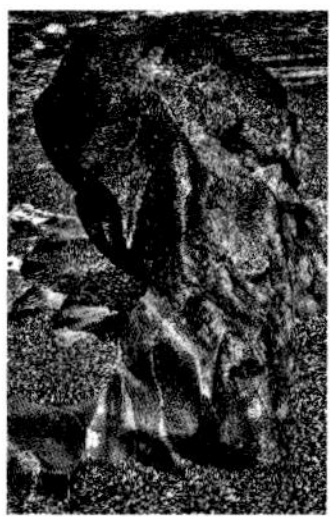
Stone Crab

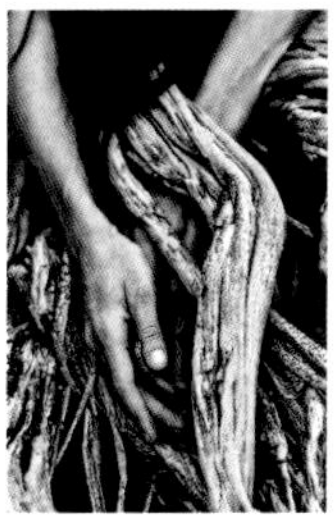
Collector

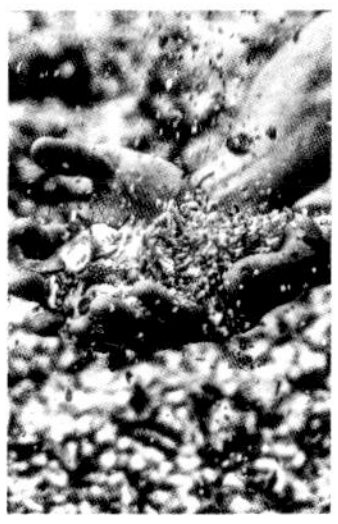
Chimes

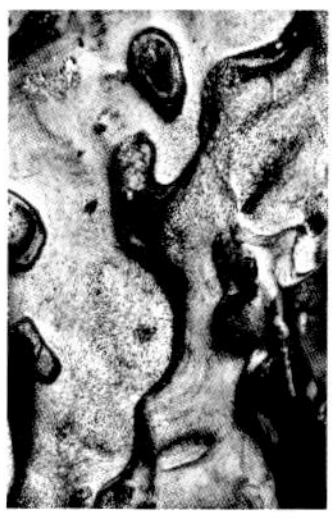
Mote

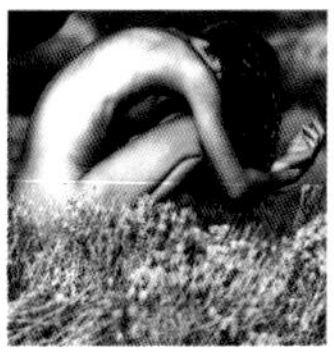
Bather

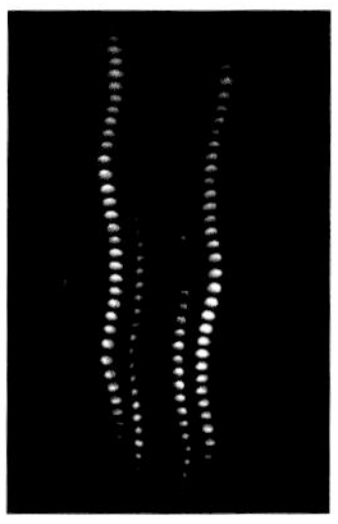
Primordial

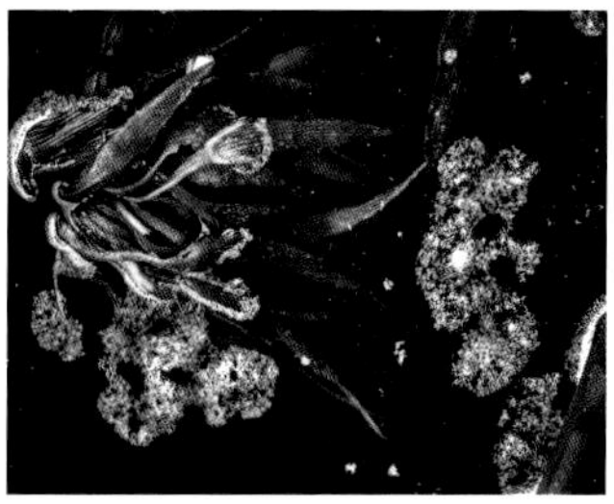
Universe

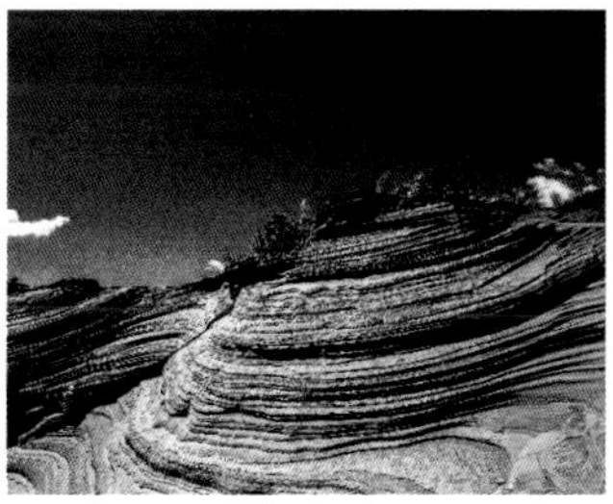
Mesa

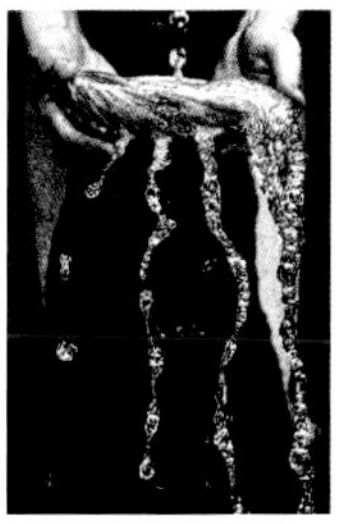
Pouring Light

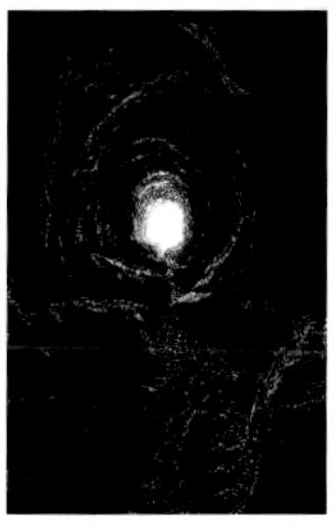
Belly of the Dragon

MYTHOSCAPE AND SPIRIT

BY CAROL HENRY

By shedding societal constraints, Azita Gandjei finds freedom to shape new realms within *Mythoscape*. Like a seed holding its secret blueprint, when her vision blooms remains unknown. With artistry, she captures humanity on a timeless stage, where her work, though seen now, may only reveal its true depth in the future.

The late, great art critic Susan Sontag refers to this in her essay "Against Interpretation" (1964). Sontag advocated, in defense of art, that what we have learned to call "form" is separated from what we call "content," though the well-intentioned statement makes "content" essential and "form" an accessory. Or as it is usually put today, a work of art, by definition, must say something. However, Sontag felt that the modern style of interpretation excavated, and as it excavates it destroys digging behind the text to find a subtext that is the true one, and *that* interpretation is the revenge of the intellect upon art. As she believed, I, too, feel that more attention lies in the "form" of art.

Azita's photographs demonstrate her keen vision through its form and transparency. Transparence means experiencing the luminosity of the thing itself, of things being what they are. Hers is the sharpness of the sensory experience and an aligning of the camera lens with the subjects, so we, too, see more and feel more.

Mythoscape is as timeless as the seed. Its mystical, dreamlike explorations intensify before the lens. Time and space are not static but transparent. The photographer Diane Arbus once said, "A photograph is a secret about a secret; the more it tells you the less you know." Exploring the *Mythoscape* book will lead to reverberations in time and space as it intensifies the dialogue between all forms. Natural forms broadly include the human form among the gestures of land and plants. The photographs are the means of conversation.

What is this reference to natural form? This journey encourages viewers on their journey to release their understanding of linear time, to surrender to a new dimension, perhaps. One where we are participants at any age or gender. Azita succeeds at placing us in each frame, one with self-nature, where time and space are one, where true time goes beyond ordinary time. To quote from a book on Zen essays, *A Flower Does Not Talk* (1970), paradise is this place of here and now. "Your going and returning take place nowhere but where you are," said Hakuin (1685–1768). The ideal "way" to enlightenment is described by the term *michi*, which translates to "abounding." The reveal in *Mythoscape* is to look around you.

That natural stage shares in a timeless Earth spirit origin. John Michell, author of *The Earth Spirit: Its Ways, Shrines, and Mysteries* (1975), states that the first people, by all accounts, lived in perfect harmony with nature and the gods. There was no punishment and fear, no judges or soldiers. The Earth gave all things spontaneously, and mankind was content with its uncultivated produce. All that life required was provided unmasked and in abundance. The Greek poet Hesiod described this as the Golden Age, an age ruled by spirits, in his piece titled *Works and Days*, written between 750 and 650 BC. The people of this age were wanderers, living under the guidance and protection of Earth spirits. They based life on the migratory paths of seasons, animals, and constellations. Time was cyclical, not linear; creation and demise were continuous, and the spirits that promoted it were eternal.

Before civilization set in, the Earth was the one universal deity. Not the material Earth, but the spirit under which, according to the ancient philosophers, lived a female creature who received the power of the sun, therefore making her animated and fertile. The spirit of the Earth is unchanging and eternal. That ancient wisdom harmonizes with Azita Gandjei's approach to the *Mythoscape* project. When she places the live participants in her oeuvre, they embrace the qualities that the Earth spirits conjure.

In this exploration of visuals set upon a timeless natural stage, there is awe-inspiring beauty shown through the selective eye of the photographer. It's a combination of earth and flesh that has formed a tolerant bond—one that we are each a part of in some way. We are the seed; we carry the map ahead to this period, collectively. It is with awareness that we proceed, hopeful.

ACKNOWLEDGMENTS

I would like to express my deepest gratitude to the many people who supported me throughout the creation of this book:

First and foremost, to my mentor, Kim Weston, whose patience and hands-off guidance were instrumental in helping me find my voice and realize my vision.

To the brilliant and talented Elizabeth Avedon and Carol Henry, whose insightful feedback and keen eye for detail helped shape the design of this book.

To the artists and models—Kaela Atleework, Vivian Cove, Mahvash Saba, and John Miller—whose talent and creativity served as a constant source of inspiration.

To the Daylight Books team, and especially Creative Director Ursula Damm, whose expertise brought the book's core message to life.

And finally, to my partner in crime, John Miller, who inspires me every day to see the world through fresh eyes. This book is dedicated to you.